PvL
1-11

more

LAST-MINUTE KNITTED GIFTS

more LAST-MINUTE KNITTED GIFTS

JOELLE HOVERSON

PHOTOGRAPHS BY ANNA WILLIAMS

STC CRAFT | A MELANIE FALICK BOOK | NEW YORK

Published in 2010 by Stewart, Tabori & Chang
An imprint of ABRAMS

Library of Congress Cataloging-in-Publication Data:
Hoverson, Joelle. More last-minute knitted gifts / Joelle Hoverson ;
photographs by Anna Williams.
p. cm.
ISBN 978-1-58479-860-6
1. Knitting--Patterns. 2. Gifts. I. Title.
TT825.H6785 2010
746.43'2041--dc22
2009035052

Editor: Melanie Falick
Designer: Brooke Hellewell Reynolds
Production Manager: Tina Cameron

The text of this book was composed in Avenir.

Printed and bound in China

10 9 8 7 6 5 4 3 2

ABRAMS
THE ART OF BOOKS SINCE 1949

115 West 18th Street
New York, NY 10011
www.abramsbooks.com

For Jen and Page,
with love and affection.

contents

introduction

As knitters, we are always looking for something more to knit, and it's always a wonderful feeling when we can spend our knitting time working on a project for someone special. After I wrote my first book, *Last-Minute Knitted Gifts*, I joked to myself that the next knitting book I would write would be called *Gifts That Take a Really Long Time to Knit*, for all of the time-consuming projects I considered creating but knew wouldn't work within the context of that book. But alas, I still have a limited amount of time to spend knitting, and I'm sure you do, too! Besides, there is nothing more satisfying than creating something beautiful and thoughtful without having to labor over it for an extended period of time.

The projects in this book are organized according to the time it took me and the knitters who helped me to complete each one. Because none of us knits at exactly the same speed, please use the times we give as guidelines rather than as hard-and-fast rules and allow extra time if you are a beginner or are knitting a larger size. To use this book, you can either pick your favorite project and find the time to make it, or you can choose a project according to the amount of time you have to work on it. The projects in the first chapter are truly fast and easy, even for less experienced knitters, whereas the projects in the last chapter are more complex and take more time. Whatever you decide to make from the following pages, rest assured that I designed every project to be a classic that will stand the test of time and that I included shortcuts or timesaving techniques in every pattern to help you finish it as quickly as possible. In some of the project introductions and in Personal Touches starting on page 10, I've included simple ideas for customizing each project for the recipient. Finally, on page 121 are some easy ideas for beautiful wrapping.

Although I can't imagine ever having the time to write my fantasy book, *Gifts That Take a Really Long Time to Knit*, I'm excited to share *More Last-Minute Knitted Gifts*. I present it with so much gratitude—for my readers, customers, friends, and family. All of you are wonderful gifts that I treasure.

personal touches

When I knit a gift, I tend to stick with a classic style that I can personalize so that it will be treasured by the recipient for a long time to come. I find the most effective and elegant way to do this is actually a simple matter of choosing the color and fiber content of my yarn with great care and consideration and sometimes adding a special stitch pattern for texture or embellishing what I've made with a very personal detail.

Color

Anyone who has met me, been to my shops, or read my other books already knows about my passion for color. For me, choosing a color for a gift for someone is in itself a symbol of my affection for them. And you can do the same. For example, if you give your sister and each member of her family a Family Ribbed Hat on page 42 in their favorite colors, or you knit your husband the Men's Zip-Up Vest on page 102 in a man-friendly neutral tone but add a zipper in a color that matches his eyes, you are showing each of them that you know and love them.

Most of the patterns in this book are knit in solid colors, which is usually my first choice since it means weaving in fewer ends (and therefore taking less time to finish!). Of course, stripes are always an easy option to add. Several of the projects are worked in a solid main color with an accent color. The Sideways Fingerless Gloves on page 49 are a perfect example. I knit this pair in two brightly contrasting colors to give to a friend who appreciates a lot of hot color in her accessories. If I had made them for someone who loves vintage style, I might have chosen an antique white for the main color and red as the contrast color (like vintage mattress ticking or antique toweling), or, alternatively, I could have knit them in one subdued color for someone who likes to keep her wardrobe understated.

Fiber

When designing these patterns, I always used the yarn that was the most inspiring to me, but selecting a yarn that is different than the one called for in the pattern is another way to customize your gift. When changing the yarn in a pattern, keep in mind that it may change the look and feel of the finished piece, but also remember that this can produce equally beautiful results. There are a couple of patterns in this book that are written for more than one yarn weight. For instance, the Beret on page 70 is written for either a fingering- or DK-weight yarn. This means that with a dozen different yarns, you can create a dozen completely different hats to suit a dozen friends, all with one pattern! When I created the hats you see here, I explored angora, wool, and even mohair, among other fibers, and while the hats are all the same shape, they all have a very different look. The instructions for the Family Ribbed Hat on page 42 cover worsted-, bulky-, and super bulky-weight yarns.

Shown clockwise from top left: Men's Zip-Up Vest (page 102), Sideways Fingerless Gloves (page 49), Family Ribbed Hat (page 42), and Berets (page 70).

Texture

If the person you are knitting for is also a knitter, she or he will most definitely appreciate carefully selected stitch patterns. The Soft as a Cloud Cowl pattern on page 99 includes three different mock cable variations, each one a little more ornate than the last. The Dreaming of Spring Fingerless Gloves pattern on page 79 includes a variation with an Aran braid along the top of the hand. Additionally, the women's version of the Toe-Up Socks on page 107 includes an optional baby cable. You can add a cable stitch to just about any pattern, but keep in mind that if your cable is very elaborate or is used across the entire piece, it will require extra yarn and will change the gauge of your piece. For example, a simple cable up the middle of the Kid's Vest on page 74 is an easy addition; all you need to do is work a swatch of the cable pattern to figure out how much it pulls in, then accommodate the difference in your cast-on.

Embellishment

One of my favorite techniques for finishing gifts with a personal touch is duplicate stitch. I used it to add initials to the Kid's Vest on page 74 and to decorate the Holiday Ornaments on page 18.

The Huggable House on page 54 is really just an excuse for embellishment. I customized the one shown with backstitch and French knots. Wouldn't it be sweet to make one to match a good friend's house? Or perhaps to create a replica of the house you grew up in to give to one of your sibling's children? Of course, you don't have to limit your French knots or backstitches to the Huggable House; they are wonderful and easy techniques that you can use to embellish any pattern in this book. For instance, imagine a neutral-colored beret covered in hot pink French knots!

Extras

Another way to personalize a knitted gift is to present it with a little something extra—such as a favorite hot beverage recipe to go with the Cozy Coasters on page 53, or perhaps a collection of embroidery supplies presented with the Soft Baskets on page 30.

Wrapping It Up

Once you've put so much thought, effort, and affection into your gift, you may not have much time leftover to think about an original way to wrap it. If this is the case, be sure to check out Wrapping Handknit Gifts on page 121.

Shown clockwise from top left: Kid's Vest (page 74), Huggable House (page 54), Soft as a Cloud Cowls (page 99), and Toe-Up Socks (page 107).

less-than-2-hour gifts

reusable hot coffee-cup sleeve

Anyone who has ever moved knows how important a good cup of coffee is on the first morning in the new place (and how challenging it can be to find the coffeepot). To lessen the drama, show up at your friend's new home with some steaming lattés in these little cozies. I used Manos del Uruguay's Wool Clásica Naturals for these because the colors reminded me of coffee with various amounts of milk. Each sleeve takes about an hour to complete.

FINISHED MEASUREMENTS
8" circumference,
at narrowest point

9 ¾" circumference,
at widest point

3 ¼" high

YARN
Manos del Uruguay Wool Clásica Naturals (100% pure wool; 138 yards / 100 grams): 1 hank #701, #702, or #703
Note: One hank will make at least 4 sleeves.

NEEDLES
One set of five double-pointed needles (dpn) size US 6 (4 mm)

Change needle size if necessary to obtain correct gauge.

NOTIONS
Stitch marker

GAUGE
18 sts and 26 rnds = 4" (10 cm) in Stockinette stitch (St st)

Sleeve
CO 36 sts. Join for working in the rnd, being careful not to twist sts; place marker (pm) for beginning of rnd.
Knit 1 rnd, purl 1 rnd.
Change to St st (knit every rnd); work even until piece measures 1 ¼" from the beginning.

Shape Sleeve
Increase Rnd 1: K1, M1, [k9, M1] 3 times, k8–40 sts. Work even until piece measures 2 ¼" from the beginning.
Increase Rnd 2: K1, M1, [k10, M1] 3 times, k9–44 sts. Work even until piece measures 3" from the beginning. Purl 1 rnd. BO all sts loosely knitwise.

holiday ornament

FINISHED MEASUREMENTS
3" diameter

YARN
Cascade Yarns Cascade 220 (100% pure new wool; 220 yards / 100 grams): 1 hank #8010 (MC). *Note: One hank will make 4 ornaments.*

Alchemy Yarns of Transformation Haiku (60% kid mohair / 40% silk; 325 yards / 25 grams): 1 hank each #44F Cherry Tart (A) and #52E Boo's Garden (B)

Alchemy Yarns of Transformation Silken Straw (100% silk; 236 yards / 40 grams): 1 hank each #39A Fuschia (C) and #50E Sour Grass (D)

NEEDLES AND NOTIONS
One set of four double-pointed needles (dpn) size US 6 (4 mm)

Crochet hook size G6 (4 mm); polyester stuffing

GAUGE
20 sts and 28 rnds = 4" (10 cm) in Stockinette stitch (St st)

CHART

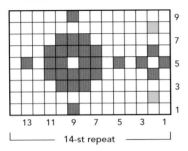

13 11 9 7 5 3 1

|—— 14-st repeat ——|

▨ One strand each of A and C held together.

▨ One strand each of B and D held together.

These festive ornaments will brighten up any home during the cold and colorless winter months. Each ornament takes about 90 minutes to knit and 30 minutes to decorate.

Ornament
Bottom Half
CO 48 sts in MC. Divide sts evenly among 3 needles. Join for working in the rnd, being careful not to twist sts.
Rnds 1 and 2: Knit.
Rnd 3: *K6, k2tog; repeat from * to end—42 sts remain.
Rnds 4 and 5: Knit.
Rnd 6: *K5, k2tog; repeat from * to end—36 sts remain.
Rnds 7 and 8: Knit.
Rnd 9: *K4, k2tog; repeat from * to end—30 sts remain.
Rnds 10 and 11: Knit.
Rnd 12: *K3, k2tog; repeat from * to end—24 sts remain.
Rnd 13: Knit.
Rnd 14: *K2, k2tog; repeat from * to end—18 sts remain.
Rnd 15: *K1, k2tog; repeat from * to end—12 sts remain.
Break yarn, leaving a 6" tail; thread tail through remaining sts, pull tight and fasten off, with tail to WS.

Top Half
With RS of Bottom Half facing, beginning at cast-on tail, pick up and knit 1 st in each cast-on st—48 sts. Work Rnds 1-15 as for Bottom Half. Break yarn, leaving a 20" long tail; thread tail through remaining sts, but do not pull closed.

Finishing
Stuff ornament to desired firmness. Pull tail tight and fasten off, but do not break yarn. Using crochet hook and tail, work crochet chain 4" long. Insert crochet hook into top of Ornament, just below first loop of crochet chain, chain 1, slip st into last st, fasten off.

Embellish Ornament with Duplicate stitch (see page 130), following photo and chart, working Rnd 5 of chart on Rnd 3 of Top Half so the repeats work out evenly.

pointy elf hat

This whimsical hat, made with a deliciously soft, naturally dyed yarn from Hand Jive, will suit any child—or adult—who dreams of being a winter elf. Even in the largest size, this project takes less than two hours from cast-on to bind-off.

SIZES
Baby (Toddler, Child/Adult Small, Adult Large)

FINISHED MEASUREMENTS
14 ½ (16 ¾, 19 ¼, 21 ½)" circumference

YARN
Hand Jive Nature's Palette Thick/Thin Bulky Merino (100% merino wool; 168 yards / 5 ounces): 1 hank Snow, Amber, Rosebud, or Sandstone. *Note: One hank will make 2 hats in sizes Baby and Toddler.*

NEEDLES
One set of four double-pointed needles (dpn) size US 13 (9 mm)

Change needle size if necessary to obtain correct gauge.

GAUGE
10 sts and 14 rnds = 4" (10 cm) in Stockinette stitch (St st)

NOTE
Since this pattern is knit entirely on double-pointed needles, you don't necessarily need a stitch marker to tell when you're at the end of the round; just look for your cast-on tail to remind you.

Hat
CO 36 (42, 48, 54) sts. Divide sts evenly among 3 needles. Join for working in the rnd, being careful not to twist sts; place marker (pm) for beginning of rnd. Begin St st (knit every rnd); work even until piece measures 4 ½ (5, 5 ½, 6)" from the beginning, with brim unrolled.

Shape Crown
Decrease Rnd: [K2tog, knit to end of needle] 3 times—33 (39, 45, 51) sts remain. Knit 1 rnd.

Repeat Decrease Rnd every other rnd 7 (10, 10, 8) times, then every rnd 3 (2, 4, 8) times—3 sts remain. Break yarn, leaving a 6" tail; thread tail through remaining sts, pull tight and fasten off, with tail to WS.

Shown from left to right: Rosebud, Snow, Amber, and Sandstone

pyramid sachet

FINISHED MEASUREMENTS
3" wide at base x 3" high

YARN
Farmhouse Yarns Bonnie's
Bamboo (100% bamboo; 200
yards / 3½ ounces): 1 hank Ivory,
Buttercup, or Gecko. *Note: One
hank will make a whole drawer-
full of sachets!*

NEEDLES
One pair straight needles size US
2 (2.75 mm) (optional)

One set of five double-pointed
needles (dpn) size US 2 (2.75 mm)

Change needle size if necessary to
obtain correct gauge.

NOTIONS
Few handfuls lavender
(see Sources for Supplies);
tapestry needle

GAUGE
15 sts and 21 rows = 3" (7.5 cm)
in Double-Knitting Pattern.
*Note: When determining your
gauge, count only the knit sts,
not the slipped sts.*

These pyramid-shaped sachets are a wonderful gift, especially for knitters who need to protect their yarn and handknits from moths. I figured out how to construct them—by double-knitting a square pouch, filling with dried lavender, and then stitching shut in a pyramid shape—by taking apart and studying a pyramid-shaped teabag. One sachet takes less than an hour to complete.

STITCH PATTERN
Double-Knitting Pattern (multiple of 2 sts; 1-row repeat)
All Rows: *K1, yf, slip 1, yb; repeat from * to end.

Sachet
Using Long-Tail CO, CO 30 sts. Begin Double-Knitting Pattern; work even until piece measures 2¾" from the beginning, ending with a WS row, with both tail and working yarn coming from the same end of the work.

Next Row (RS): *Slip 1 st to front dpn, slip 1 st to back dpn; repeat from * to end. Redistribute sts as follows to prepare for finishing: K7 from front needle onto new dpn (Needle 1), k8 from front needle onto second new dpn (Needle 2), k7 from back needle onto Needle 2, k8 from back needle onto Needle 1.

Finishing
Fill sachet with lavender.
Using Kitchener st (see page 128), graft sts together, leaving a 10" tail.

Tassel
Cut four 7" strands of yarn. Using a tapestry needle, thread strands through st just below tail from grafting, leaving a 3½" strand on either side of st. Gather strands together and wrap tail around strands for ½" from point of Pyramid. Secure tail through center of tassel and into Sachet. Trim excess yarn.

seed-stitch bracelet

If you've got 30 minutes to spare, you can whip up one of these bracelets for your best friend, mother, sister, or even yourself. One hank of Koigu's Mori will make at least eight bracelets (not including the stripe, of course). Every woman at our photo shoot requested a bracelet to take home, so I already know they're crowd-pleasers.

FINISHED MEASUREMENTS
6¾" wide x 1" long

YARN
Koigu Mori (50% merino wool / 50% mulberry silk; 185 yards / 50 grams): Small amount of #M2360 (MC). *Note: One hank of this yarn will make about 8 bracelets.*

Koigu Premium Merino (100% merino wool; 175 yards / 50 grams): Small amounts of color of your choice (A)

NEEDLES
One pair straight needles size US 1 (2.25 mm)

Change needle size if necessary to obtain correct gauge.

NOTIONS
One ⅜" button; sewing needle and cotton thread (for attaching button)

GAUGE
32 sts and 44 rows = 4" (10 cm) in Seed stitch

STITCH PATTERN
Seed Stitch (multiple of 2 sts + 1; 1-row repeat)
All Rows: K1, *p1, k1; repeat from * to end.

Bracelet
Using MC, CO 55 sts. Begin Seed st; work even for 4 rows. Change to A; work even for 1 row.
Buttonhole Row (WS): K1, p1, k2tog, yo, work to end.
Next Row (RS): Change to MC; work even for 5 rows. BO all sts loosely in pattern.

Finishing
Block if desired. Sew button at opposite end from buttonhole.

linen-stitch bookmark

FINISHED MEASUREMENTS
1 3/8" wide x 7" long

YARN
Alchemy Yarns of Transformation Juniper (100% superfine merino; 232 yards / 50 grams): 1 hank #21E Green Plum, #95M Mica, #65E Dragon, #17E Sweet Lime, or #23E Good Earth. *Note: One hank will make at least 8 solid-color bookmarks.*

NEEDLES
One pair straight needles size US 4 (3.5 mm)

Change needle size if necessary to obtain correct gauge.

GAUGE
16 sts and 30 rows = 2" (5 cm) in Linen stitch

NOTE
If you want to make a multicolored Bookmark, simply change colors as desired.

I've always been a huge fan of linen stitch; in fact, the finer the yarn, the more I love it. But linen stitch is time-consuming, so I usually reserve it for small projects like these bookmarks. In beautiful shades of green, they're a perfect gift for a gardener who reads and dreams about plants all winter. The yarn is Juniper, a fine, washable merino from Alchemy. When I look at these colors, I can tell that Gina Wilde (Alchemy's owner and amazing master dyer) spends a lot of time in her garden.

STITCH PATTERN
Linen Stitch (multiple of 2 sts + 1; 2-row repeat)
Row 1 (RS): K1, *slip 1 wyif, k1; repeat from * to end.
Row 2: K1, p1, *slip 1 wyib, p1; repeat from * to last st, k1.
Repeat Rows 1 and 2 for Linen Stitch.

Bookmark
CO 11 sts. Begin Linen St; work even until piece measures 7" from the beginning, ending with a WS row.
BO Row (RS): K1, *p1, pass last st over, k1, pass last st over; repeat from * to end. Fasten off.

Finishing
Block if desired.

2 - to 4 -hour gifts

soft baskets

SIZES
Small (Medium, Large)

FINISHED MEASUREMENTS
Approximately 4½ (5½, 6½)"
square at base x 4" high, with
ribbing folded over

YARN
Blue Sky Alpacas Cotton (100%
cotton; 150 yards /100 grams):
1 hank #80 Bone (Small), #82 Nut
(Medium), and #639 Wasabi (Large)

NEEDLES
One pair straight needles size US
7 (4.5 mm)

One 16" (40 cm) long circular (circ)
needle size US 7 (4.5 mm)

Change needle size if necessary to
obtain correct gauge.

NOTIONS
Stitch markers

GAUGE
17 sts and 24 rows = 4" (10 cm) in
Stockinette stitch (St st)

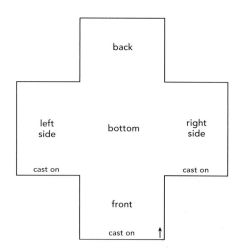

I made and remade these baskets many times using all sorts of contortions and techniques, until I finally succeeded with this easy and satisfying pattern. A charming gift for a crafty friend with lots of notions or other small treasures floating around!

STITCH PATTERN
1x1 Rib (multiple of 2 sts; 1-rnd repeat)
All Rnds: *K1, p1; repeat from * to end.

NOTE
The Baskets are worked in one piece, beginning with the Front, casting on stitches for the Right and Left Sides, working across the Bottom to the base of the Back, where the Right and Left Side stitches are bound-off, then up the Back (see Diagram).

Front
Using straight needles, CO 20 (24, 28) sts. Begin St st; work even for 3", ending with a RS row. Knit 1 row (turning row).

Bottom and Right and Left Sides
Next Row (RS): Using Cable CO (see page 131), CO 13 sts, knit across 12 CO sts, pm, knit to end—46 (50, 54) sts.
Next Row: CO 13 sts, purl across 13 CO sts, pm, purl to end.
Row 1 (RS): [Knit to marker, slip marker, slip 1] twice, knit to end.
Row 2: Purl.
Repeat Rows 1 and 2 until piece measures 4½ (5½, 6½)" from last CO row.

Back
Next Row (RS): BO 13 sts, removing marker, knit to end—33 (37, 41) sts remain.
Repeat last row once (turning row)—20 (24, 28) sts remain.
Continuing in St st, work even for 3", ending with a WS row. BO all sts.

Finishing
Sew side seams.
Top Band: Using circ needle, pick up and knit 19 (23, 27) sts between seams on each side—76 (92, 108) sts. Join for working in the rnd; pm for beginning of rnd. Begin 1x1 Rib; work even for 2". BO all sts in pattern. Fold BO edge to RS. Fill with goodies!

movie star scarf

This small scarf is quick, relatively easy to make, lightweight enough to wear almost any day of the year—and very glamorous. I have a vision in my head of Grace Kelly wearing one just like it while driving in a convertible. I don't know if my vision comes from a scene in one of her movies or if I made it up. If you use the yarn I did—Mooi by Louet—you'll be able to make five scarves out of just one hank. Imagine you and four of your friends all looking like movie stars!

FINISHED MEASUREMENTS
4" wide x 23" long at longest point, after blocking

YARN
Louet Mooi Lace Weight (70% bamboo / 15% bison / 15% cashmere; 350 yards / 50 grams): 1 hank #16 Spring Aqua. *Note: One hank will make 5 scarves!*

NEEDLES
One pair straight needles size US 5 (3.75 mm)

Three double-pointed needles (dpn) size US 5 (3.75 mm)

Change needle size if necessary to obtain correct gauge.

GAUGE
32 sts and 36 rows = 4" (10 cm) in Stockinette stitch (St st)

STITCH PATTERN

1x1 Rib (multiple of 2 sts; 1-row repeat)

All Rows: *K1, p1; repeat from * to end.

Scarf
CO 32 sts.
Row 1 (RS): K1-f/b, knit to last 2 sts, k2tog.
Row 2: Purl.
Repeat Rows 1 and 2 until piece measures 4" from the beginning, ending with a WS row.

Shape Keyhole
Next Row (RS): *Slip 1 st to front dpn, slip 1 st to back dpn; repeat from * to end. Set aside sts on back dpn. Working only on sts on front dpn, change to 1x1 Rib; work even for 1", ending with a WS row. Set aside.
Next Row (RS): Rejoin yarn to sts on back dpn; work as for sts on front dpn.

Rejoin Keyhole
Next Row (RS): *K1 from front dpn, k1 from back dpn; repeat from * to end–32 sts. Continuing in St st, work even until piece measures 17" from the beginning, or to 5" less than desired length.
Decrease Row (RS): *K2tog, p2tog; repeat from * to end–16 sts remain.
Change to 1x1 Rib; work even for 1", ending with a WS row.
Increase Row (RS): *K1-f/b; repeat from * to end–32 sts. Purl 1 row.
Row 1 (RS): K2tog, knit to last st, k1-f/b.
Row 2: Purl.
Repeat Rows 1 and 2 for 4", ending with a WS row. BO all sts.

Finishing
Block as desired.

baby socks

SIZE
0-6 (6-9, 9-12) months

FINISHED MEASUREMENTS
3 ¾" foot circumference

3 ¾ (4 ¼, 4 ½)" foot length from
back of heel

YARN
Jade Sapphire Zageo 6-Ply
Cashmere (100% Mongolian
cashmere; 150 yards / 55 grams):
1 hank Tanis Grey, Peach Honey,
or Verdigris

NEEDLES
One set of four double-pointed
needles (dpn) size US 4 (3.5 mm)

Change needle size if necessary to
obtain correct gauge.

NOTIONS
Stitch marker

GAUGE
13 sts and 16 rnds = 2" (5 cm) in
Stockinette stitch (St st)

Socks are super-quick when baby-sized—in this case, about 3 hours per pair. For yarn, I chose Jade Sapphire's Zageo 6-ply cashmere, but about 90 yards of any DK or light worsted-weight yarn will do as long as you can get the correct gauge.

Leg
CO 24 sts. Divide sts among 3 needles (6-6-12). Join for working in the rnd, being careful not to twist sts; place marker (pm) for beginning of rnd. Begin St st (knit every rnd); work even until piece measures 2 (2 ¼, 2 ½)" from the beginning (unrolled).

Heel Flap
Set-Up Row (WS): Turn, p12. Leave remaining 12 sts on 2 needles for instep.
Row 1 (RS): Working only on 12 Heel Flap sts, *slip 1, k1; repeat from * to end.
Row 2: Slip 1, purl to end.
Repeat Rows 1 and 2 five times.

Turn Heel
Set-Up Row 1: K6, ssk, k1, turn.
Set-Up Row 2: Slip 1, p1, p2tog, p1, turn.
Row 1: Slip 1, knit to 1 st before gap, ssk [the 2 sts on either side of gap], k1, turn.
Row 2: Slip 1, purl to 1 st before gap, p2tog [the 2 sts on either side of gap], p1, turn.
Repeat Rows 1 and 2 once, omitting final k1 and p1 sts in second repeat of Rows 1 and 2—6 sts remain.

Gusset
Note: When picking up sts, pick up both legs of each st picked up; this will help to minimize the gap.
Next Rnd: Needle 1: Knit across Heel Flap sts, pick up and knit 6 sts along left side of Heel Flap; Needle 2: Knit 12 sts for instep onto 1 needle; Needle 3: Pick up and knit 6 sts along right side of heel flap, k3 from Needle 1; pm for beginning of rnd—30 sts (9-12-9).
Decrease Rnd: Needle 1: Knit to last 3 sts, k2tog, k1; Needle 2: Knit; Needle 3: K1, ssk, knit to end—28 sts remain. Work even for 1 rnd.
Repeat Decrease Rnd every other rnd twice—24 sts remain (6-12-6).

Foot

Work even until Foot measures 3 (3 ½, 3 ¾)" from back of Heel.

Toe

Decrease Rnd: Needle 1: Knit to last 3 sts, k2tog, k1; Needle 2: K1, ssk, knit to last 3 sts, k2tog, k1; Needle 3: K1, ssk, knit to end–20 sts remain. Knit 1 rnd.
Repeat Decrease Rnd every other rnd twice–12 sts remain (3-6-3). Knit sts from Needle 1 onto Needle 3.

Finishing

Break yarn, leaving long tail. Using Kitchener st (see page 128), graft Toe sts.
Block if desired.

Shown clockwise from top:
Tanis Grey, Peach Honey, and Verdigris

baby bonnet

I love that this bonnet is constructed without any seams. You cast on at the bottom end of the chin strap and work your way up and over the head and back down to the button on the opposite side. The style works for boys and girls, so you can start it before the baby is born even if you don't know the sex, as long as you choose your color carefully.

FINISHED MEASUREMENTS
12" from bottom edge to bottom edge, over top of head

12" at base of neck, unbuttoned, not including Strap

YARN
Lobster Pot Yarns Worsted Hand-Dyed Cashmere (100% cashmere; 100 yards / 50 grams): 1 hank Chatham Light

NEEDLES
One pair straight needles or one 16" (40 cm) long circular needle size US 9 (5.5 mm)

Change needle size if necessary to obtain correct gauge.

NOTIONS
Stitch markers; one ¾" button

GAUGE
14 sts and 20 rows = 4" (10 cm) in Stockinette stitch (St st)

Strap
CO 5 sts. Begin Garter st (knit every row). Work even for 2 rows.
Buttonhole Row (RS): K2, yo, k2tog, k1.
Work even until piece measures 7" from the beginning, ending with a WS row. Do not turn work.

Hat
With WS of Strap facing, pick up and knit 6 sts along left-hand edge of Strap, just below needle—11 sts. Knit 2 rows.

Shape Hat
Increase Row 1 (RS): K5, [M1-r, M1-l] into same strand, k1, M1-l, k5—14 sts.
Next Row: K5, p4, k5.
Increase Row 2: K5, M1-r, place marker (pm), k2, M1-l, k1, pm, M1-l, knit to end—17 sts.
Next Row: K5, purl to last 5 sts, knit to end.
Increase Row 3: Knit to first marker, M1-r, slip marker (sm), k2, M1-l, knit to next marker, sm, M1-l, knit to end—20 sts. Work even for 1 row, working increased sts in St st.
Repeat Increase Row 3 every other row 9 times—47 sts. Work even for 3", ending with a RS row, and removing markers on last row.
Next Row (WS): Work 18 sts, pm, work 12 sts, pm, work to end.
Decrease Row 1 (RS): Work to 2 sts before marker, k2tog, sm, ssk, work to next marker, sm, ssk, work to end—44 sts remain. Work even for 1 row.
Repeat Decrease Row 1 every other row 10 times—14 sts remain. Work even for 1 row, removing all markers.
Decrease Row 2: K5, k2tog, ssk, k5—12 sts remain. Work even for 1 row.
Decrease Row 3: K2, k2tog, ssk, knit to end—10 sts remain. Knit 1 row.
Decrease Row 4: K4, skp, turn, knit to end—9 sts remain.
Repeat Decrease Row 4 every other row 4 times—5 sts remain. BO all sts.

Finishing
Sew button to Strap at opposite end from buttonhole, adjusting position of button if necessary for more comfortable fit. Block if desired.

big lace scarf

FINISHED MEASUREMENTS
11 ½" wide x 45" long

YARN
Cascade Yarns Magnum (100% wool; 123 yards / 250 grams): 1 hank #9452

NEEDLES
One pair straight needles size US 17 (12.75 mm)

Change needle size if necessary to obtain correct gauge.

GAUGE
7 sts and 9 rows = 4" (10 cm) in Openwork Pattern

This is a fantastic last-minute project. It takes only one hank of yarn. And it's big, soft, beautiful, and easy—perfect when you're in a hurry but still want to create something special.

STITCH PATTERN
Openwork Pattern (multiple of 6 sts + 2; 4-row repeat)
Row 1 (RS): K1, *k3, yo, sk2p, yo; repeat from * to last st, k1.
Row 2: Purl.
Row 3: K1, *yo, sk2p, yo, k3; repeat from * to last st, k1.
Row 4: Purl.
Repeat Rows 1-4 for Openwork Pattern.

Scarf
CO 20 sts. Begin Openwork Pattern; work even until yarn is nearly gone, leaving enough yarn to BO. BO all sts loosely.

Finishing
Block if desired.

family ribbed hats

This hat is my response to the countless knitters who have come into our shop over the years and requested a simple, easy pattern for a hat that fits just about anyone. This pattern, which includes instructions for three different yarn weights, works for men, women, teenagers, and children. The circumference of these hats is nearly the same for each size. They are elastic enough that they will stretch to fit any size head. Only the length is different from one size to the next.

SIZES
Child, Woman, Man

NOTIONS
Stitch marker

Worsted Weight

FINISHED MEASUREMENTS
14" circumference

YARN
Jade Sapphire 100% Mongolian Cashmere 6 Ply (55 grams / 150 yards): 135 (160, 180) yards Peach Honey or Green Tea

NEEDLES
One 16" (40 cm) long circular (circ) needle size US 3 (3.25 mm)

One set of five double-pointed needles (dpn) size US 3 (3.25 mm)

GAUGE
32 sts and 32 rnds = 4" (10 cm) in 2x2 Rib, unstretched

Heavy Worsted / Bulky Weight

FINISHED MEASUREMENTS
13 ¾" circumference

YARN
Jade Sapphire 100% Mongolian Cashmere 8 Ply (55 grams / 100 yards): 115 (130, 150) yards Black Walnut

NEEDLES
One 16" (40 cm) long circular (circ) needle size US 5 (3.75 mm)

One set of five double-pointed needles (dpn) size US 5 (3.75 mm)

GAUGE
28 sts and 28 rnds = 4" (10 cm) in 2x2 Rib, unstretched

Bulky / Super Bulky Weight

FINISHED MEASUREMENTS
13" circumference

YARN
Jade Sapphire 100% Mongolian Cashmere 12 Ply (55 grams / 60 yards): 70 (80, 90) yards Ivory or Driftwood

NEEDLES
One 16" (40 cm) long circular (circ) needle size US 10 (6 mm)

One set of five double-pointed needles (dpn) size US 10 (6 mm)

GAUGE
22 sts and 24 rnds = 4" (10 cm) in 2x2 Rib, unstretched

Note: If you would like to substitute another yarn for the yarn used here, choose a yarn with the following Stockinette stitch (St st) gauge:

Worsted Weight:
18-20 sts = 4" (10 cm)

Heavy Worsted / Bulky Weight:
14-16 sts = 4" (10 cm)

Bulky / Super Bulky Weight:
10-12 sts = 4" (10 cm)

STITCH PATTERNS

2x2 Rib (multiple of 4 sts; 1-rnd repeat)
All Rnds: *K2, p2; repeat from * to end.

1x1 Rib (multiple of 2 sts; 1-rnd repeat)
All Rnds: *K1, p1; repeat from * to end.

NOTE
Instructions for Worsted Weight are given first, with instructions for Heavy Worsted/Bulky Weight and Bulky/Super Bulky Weight in parentheses. When only one figure is given, it applies to all gauges.

Hat
Using circ needle CO 112 (96, 72) sts. Join for working in the rnd, being careful not to twist sts; place marker (pm) for beginning of rnd. Begin 2x2 rib; work even until piece measures 5 ½" for Child's size, 6 ½" for Women's size, or 7 ½" for Men's size.

Shape Crown
Note: Change to dpns when necessary for number of sts on needle.
Decrease Rnd 1: *K2tog, p2tog; repeat from * to end—56 (48, 36) sts remain.
Next Rnd: Change to 1x1 Rib; work even for 4 rnds.
Decrease Rnd 2: *K2tog; repeat from * to end—28 (24, 18) sts remain. Knit 1 rnd.
Next Rnd: Repeat Decrease Rnd 2—14 (12, 9) sts remain.
Break yarn, leaving 8" long tail. Thread tail through remaining sts, pull tight and fasten off.

Shown clockwise from top right: Green Tea in Worsted, Ivory in Super Bulky, Peach Honey in Worsted, Black Walnut in Bulky, Driftwood in Super Bulky

4 - to 6 -hour gifts

sideways fingerless gloves

SIZES
Women's X-Small (Small, Medium, Large, 1X-Large)

FINISHED MEASUREMENTS
6 (6 ½, 7, 7 ½, 8)" circumference

YARN
Jade Sapphire 2-Ply Cashmere Silk (55% silk / 45% cashmere; 400 yards / 55 grams): 1 hank each #073 Bougainvillea (A) and #107 Masala (B)

NEEDLES
One pair straight needles size US 4 (3.5 mm)

Change needle size if necessary to obtain correct gauge.

NOTIONS
Crochet hook size US E/4 (3.5 mm) and smooth waste yarn (if using Provisional CO; see Notes); stitch marker

GAUGE
24 sts and 32 rows = 4" (10 cm) in Stockinette stitch (St st), using 2 strands of yarn held together

I based these funky-feminine fingerless gloves on a pair that my sister Jen gave me for Christmas a few years ago. They came from Dosa, one of my favorite stores in Manhattan (conveniently located in the same neighborhood as my shop). I wore them so often that they were nearly threadbare, so I decided to create another pair as an homage to the first. I worked with Jade Sapphire's 2-Ply Cashmere Silk, doubled, swapping in a second color for one of the strands of yarn at the top of the hand; the two skeins required make at least two pairs.

STITCH PATTERN
Seed Stitch (multiple of 2 sts + 1; 1-row repeat)
All Rows: *K1, p1; repeat from * to last st, k1.

NOTES
Gloves are worked from side to side, beginning at the outside edge of the hand.

If working a Provisional Cast-On and Kitchener stitch are keeping you from making this project, you can cast on with a regular Long-Tail Cast-On (see page 131) and bind off loosely, then sew the cast-on and bound-off edges together.

Right Glove

Back of Hand

With 2 strands of A held together, using Provisional (Crochet Chain) CO (see page 132), CO 41 (45, 45, 49, 49) sts. Purl 1 row.

Eyelet Row (WS): *P2tog, yo; repeat from * to last st, k1.

Next Row: Change to 1 strand each of A and B held together. Work 3 sts in Seed st, work in St st to last 3 sts, work in Seed st to end. Work even until piece measures 2 ½ (2 ¾, 3, 3 ¼, 3 ½)" from the beginning, ending with a WS row. Change to 2 strands of A held together. Work even until piece measures 3 (3 ¼, 3 ½, 3 ¾, 4)" from the beginning, ending with a WS row.

Thumb Opening

Next Row (RS): Work 19 (21, 21, 23, 23) sts in Seed st, work in St st to last 3 sts, work in Seed st to end. Work even for 1 row.

Next Row (RS): Work 7 (9, 9, 11, 11) sts, BO next 9 sts loosely in pattern, work to end. Work even for 2 rows, CO 9 sts over BO sts on first row, using Cable CO (see page 131).

Palm

Next Row (WS): Work 3 sts in Seed st, work in St st to last 3 sts, work in Seed st to end. Work even until piece measures 5 ¾ (6 ¼, 6 ¾, 7 ¼, 7 ¾)" from the beginning, ending with a RS row.

Eyelet Row (WS): *K2tog, yo; repeat from * to last st, k1. Purl 1 row. Leave sts on needle for finishing.

Finishing

Carefully unravel Provisional CO and place sts on needle. With WS facing, using Kitchener st (see page 128), graft edges together. Turn Glove RS out. Block if desired.

Left Glove

Work as for Right Glove to beginning of Thumb Opening.

Thumb Opening

Next Row (RS): Work 3 sts in Seed st, work 19 (21, 21, 23, 23) sts in St st, work in Seed st to end. Work even for 1 row.

Next Row (RS): Work 25 (27, 27, 29, 29) sts, BO next 9 sts loosely, work to end. Work even for 2 rows, CO 9 sts over BO sts on first row, using Cable CO.

Complete as for Right Glove.

cozy coasters

These coasters make a warm and rich housewarming gift, especially when presented with a little something extra, such as a special tea or the ingredients and recipe for another hot beverage. They are double-knit with two colors, which means they look nearly identical on both sides. The first two rows on each side can be a little tricky to keep track of, but once you've got the pattern established, it flows right along. A set of two takes about four hours to finish.

FINISHED MEASUREMENTS
Approximately 3 ½" square

YARN
Blue Sky Alpacas Melange (100% baby alpaca; 110 yards / 50 grams): 1 hank #809 Toasted Almond (A); 1 hank #803 Licorice, #804 Cinnamon, #805 Huckleberry, #806 Salsa, #807 Dijon, #813 Pomegranate, or #814 Pumpernickel (B)

NEEDLES
One pair double-pointed needles (dpn) size US 7 (4.5 mm)

Change needle size if necessary to obtain correct gauge.

GAUGE
37 ½ sts and 15 knit column rows in A (30 working rows) = 3" (7.5 cm) in Double-Knit Pattern

Shown clockwise from top right: Toasted Almond paired with Pumpernickel, Huckleberry, Pomegranate, Cinnamon, Salsa, Dijon, and Licorice

STITCH PATTERN
Double-Knit Pattern (multiple of 4 sts; 2-row repeat)

Note: The letter following the row number indicates the color to be used when working that row.

Row 1 B: Bring yarn to front, over A to twist strands, *k1, yf, slip 1, yb, slip 1, yf, slip 1, yb; repeat from * to end. Do not turn work; slide sts to opposite end of needle.
Row 1 A: With A, *yb, slip 1, yf, slip 1, yb, k1, yf, slip 1; repeat from * to end. Turn work.
Repeat Rows 1 B and 1 A for Double-Knit Pattern.

NOTES
This pattern is double-knit, which results in a fabric that is knit on both sides. Each row is worked in two passes, the first pass with B and the second pass with A.

When changing from A to B at the beginning of Row 1 B, twist the strands once to prevent a hole.

Coaster
Using A, CO 44 sts. Begin Double-Knit Pattern; work even until piece measures 3¼" from the beginning, ending with Row 1 B.
Next Row A: *K1, slip 1 wyif; repeat from * to end. Continuing in A, repeat last row once.
BO Row A: K2tog, *k2tog, pass first st on right-hand needle over second and off needle; repeat from * to end. Fasten off.

Finishing
Block as desired.

huggable house

I've always loved the process of creating something dimensional out of something that is essentially flat, so making this house was a real treat for me. It's so satisfying to sew together those flat pieces, then stuff and watch the whole thing come to life right before your eyes. Make it any color and embellish it to your heart's content.

FINISHED MEASUREMENTS
Approximately 5" square at base x 9" tall

YARN
Cascade Yarns Cascade 220 (100% wool; 220 yards / 100 grams): 1 hank each #8010 (MC) and #2401 (A)

Paternayan Persian Yarn (100% Persian virgin wool; 8 yards): 1 hank each #420 (B), #556 (C), #760 (D), #770 (E), #960 (F), and #697 (G)

NEEDLES
One pair straight needles size US 6 (4 mm)

Change needle size if necessary to obtain correct gauge.

NOTIONS
Tapestry needle; polyester stuffing

GAUGE
22 sts and 28 rows = 4" (10 cm) in Stockinette stitch (St st)

STITCH PATTERN
Seed Stitch (odd number of sts; 1-row repeat)
All Rows: K1, *p1, k1; repeat from * to end.

NOTE
The House begins at the peak of the Front gable, works down to the base of the Front, across the Bottom, then up to the peak of the Back gable. The Right Side is picked up from the Bottom, worked up and over the Roof, then down the Left Side to the Bottom.

Front
Using MC, CO 3 sts.
Increase Row 1 (RS): K1-f/b, k1, k1-f/b—5 sts. Purl 1 row.
Increase Row 2 (RS): K1, k1-f/b, knit to last 2 sts, k1-f/b, k1—7 sts. Purl 1 row.
Repeat Increase Row 2 every other row 11 times—29 sts.
Work even for 5", ending with a WS row. Purl 1 row (turning row).

Bottom
Work even in St st for 5", ending with a WS row. Purl 1 row (turning row).

Back
Work even in St st for 5", ending with a WS row.
Decrease Row 1 (RS): K1, ssk, knit to last 3 sts, k2tog, k1—27 sts remain. Purl 1 row.
Repeat Decrease Row 1 every other row 11 times—5 sts remain.
Decrease Row 2 (RS): K1, ssk, k2tog—3 sts remain. Break yarn, leaving a 6" tail. Thread tail through remaining sts, pull tight and fasten off.

Right Side
With RS facing, using MC, pick up and knit 29 sts along 1 side of Bottom, being careful to pick up sts between turning rows. Begin St st; work even for 5", ending with a WS row.

Roof

Change to A and Seed st; work even until piece measures 4" from color change, ending with a WS row. Purl 1 row (turning row). Work even in Seed st until piece measures 4" from turning row, ending with a RS row. Change to MC; work even for 1 row.

Left Side

Change to St st; work even for 5" from color change. BO all sts, leaving a long tail for finishing.

Finishing

Using MC and Mattress st (see page 126), sew Side and Roof seams, leaving 1 side of Roof unsewn for stuffing. Stuff House until plump. Sew final seam.

Embroidering Huggable House

Using B and Backstitch, outline door and window frames. Using B and Duplicate st (see page 130), work doorknob (see photo). Using C, fill in window panes (see photo). Using D, E, F, and G, work French knots for flowers along bottom edge of window and bottom perimeter of House (see photo).

Backstitch

Step 1: Place 4 safety pins or removable stitch markers to define the corners of the window or door.

Step 2: Cut a length of yarn no longer than your arm and thread a tapestry needle, leaving a tail approximately 5" long; do not tie a knot at the end of yarn.

Step 3: Insert the needle from the right side of the House down through the knitted fabric a few inches away from the marked stitch, then come up 2 stitches below the marked stitch, keeping in line vertically with the marked stitch. Pull the yarn through gently, leaving approximately 3" of yarn inside the stuffing.

Step 4: Insert the needle into the end of the previous stitch and bring it back out 2 stitches below where your yarn emerges from the surface (see photo at top right).

Repeat Step 4 until you come to the second marker. Work the horizontal stitches the same way, as seen in the photo at bottom right.

Step 5: When you are through, insert the tapestry needle into the last stitch and come out a few inches away, pull the yarn tight and trim the excess yarn, allowing the tail to disappear into the stuffing.

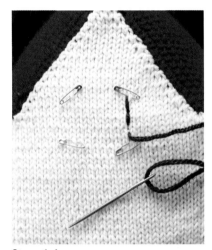

Steps 1-4

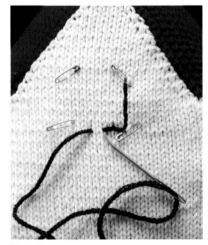

Step 4

French Knots

Step 1: Cut a length of yarn no longer than your arm and thread a tapestry needle, leaving a tail approximately 5" long; do not tie a knot in the end of the yarn.

Step 2: Insert the needle from the right side of the House a few inches away from where you'd like your first knot to be, pull the needle back out where you'd like your first knot to be, pull the yarn through, leaving a tail approximately 5" long, to be woven in when you are through.

Step 3: Wrap the yarn around the needle twice, close to where you came out of the knitting, as shown in the top photo at right.

Step 4: *Insert the needle back into the fabric next to the stitch where it originally came out, then push the needle back up through the knitting to where you'd like your next knot to be, as in the photo at bottom right. Pull the yarn through, holding the wrapped yarn securely until you have pulled the entire length through.

Repeat Step 4 until you have worked as many French knots as you would like.

Step 5: When you are through, trim the excess yarn, allowing the tail to disappear into the stuffing.

Steps 1-3

Step 4

kelly's mittens

SIZES
Women's Small (Medium, Large)

FINISHED MEASUREMENTS
6 ¾ (7 ½, 8 ½)" circumference

YARN
Blue Sky Alpacas Brushed Suri
(67% baby Suri alpaca / 22%
merino wool / 11% bamboo;
142 yards / 50 grams): 1 hank
#900 Whipped Cream (A)

Blue Sky Alpacas Suri Merino
(60% baby Suri alpaca / 40%
merino wool; 164 yards / 100
grams): 1 hank #410 Snow (B)

NEEDLES
One set of four double-pointed
needles (dpn) size US 6 (4 mm)

One set of four double-pointed
needles size US 5 (3.75 mm)

Change needle size if necessary to
obtain correct gauge.

NOTIONS
Stitch marker; waste yarn

GAUGE
17 sts and 20 rnds = 4" (10 cm) in
Brioche Stitch, using 2 strands of
A held together

21 sts and 28 rnds = 4" (10 cm)
in Stockinette stitch (St st) (knit
every rnd), using 2 strands of B
held together

Before I learned how to knit, I would watch my friend Kelly McKaig in fascination as she knit mitten after mitten on double-pointed needles, all the while telling me that I could do it, too. I didn't believe her at the time, but now of course I am so thankful for her encouragement. Here is one of Kelly's patterns—with a special detail, a Suri alpaca brioche-stitch cuff.

ABBREVIATIONS
RLI (right lifted increase): Pick up st below next st on left-hand needle and place on left-hand needle; knit the picked-up st.

LLI (left lifted increase): Pick up st below last st on right-hand needle and place on left-hand needle; knit the picked-up st through the back loop.

STITCH PATTERN
Brioche Stitch (multiple of 2 sts; 2-rnd repeat)
Set-Up Rnd: *Yo, slip 1, k1; repeat from * to end.
Rnd 1: *P2tog (yo from previous rnd together with following st), slip 1, yo; repeat from * to end.
Rnd 2: *Yo, slip 1, k2tog (next st together with yo from previous rnd); repeat from * to end.
Repeat Rnds 1 and 2 for Brioche Stitch.

NOTE
To work a yo at the beginning of a needle, bring the yarn forward (to the purl position). Keeping the yarn in front of the working (empty) needle, slip the first stitch, then bring the yarn over the needle and to the back when you work k1 or k2tog on the following stitch(es).

Cuff
Using larger needles and 2 strands of A held together, CO 26 (28, 30) sts. Divide sts among 3 needles [8-8-10 (8-10-10, 10-10-10)]. Join for working in the rnd, being careful not to twist sts; place marker (pm) for beginning of rnd. Begin Brioche Stitch; work even until piece measures 4" from the beginning. Knit 1 rnd, knitting into the back of yo's to close holes, and decreasing 3 (2, 3) sts evenly—36 (40, 42) sts remain. Change to smaller needles, B, and St st (knit every rnd); work even for 4 rnds.

Thumb Gusset

Increase Rnd 1: LLI, k1, RLI, pm, knit to end of rnd–38 (42, 44) sts. Work even for 2 rnds.

Increase Rnd 2: LLI, knit to marker, RLI, slip marker (sm), knit to end–40 (44, 46) sts. Work even for 2 rnds.

Repeat Increase Rnd 2 every 3 rnds 4 times–48 (52, 54) sts. Work even for 2 rnds.

Divide for Thumb: Work 13 sts and place on waste yarn for Thumb, removing second marker, knit to end, CO 1 (1, 3) st(s) using Cable CO (see page 131)—36 (40, 44) sts remain.

Hand

Continuing in St st, work even for 4½", or to 1" less than desired length to Mitten Top.

Mitten Top

Decrease Rnd 1: *K2, k2tog; repeat from * to end–27 (30, 33) sts remain. Work even for 2 rnds.

Decrease Rnd 2: *K1, k2tog; repeat from * to end–18 (20, 22) sts remain. Work even for 2 rnds.

Decrease Rnd 3: *K2tog; repeat from * to end–9 (10, 11) sts remain. Cut yarn, leaving 8" tail. Thread tail through remaining sts, pull tight, and fasten off.

Thumb

Transfer 13 sts from waste yarn to 2 smaller dpns [4-9]. Rejoin yarn.

Rnd 1: With third dpn, pick up and knit 3 (3, 5) sts from gap, knit to end; pm for beginning of rnd–16 (16, 18) sts. Work even for 2 rnds.

Size Large Only

Decrease Rnd: K2, k2tog, knit to end–17 sts remain. Work even for 2 rnds.

Repeat Decrease Rnd once–16 sts remain.

All Sizes

Working in St st, work even until piece measures 2" from picked-up sts.

Decrease Rnd 1: *K2, k2tog; repeat from * to end–12 sts remain. Work even for 2 rnds.

Decrease Rnd 2: *K1, k2tog; repeat from * to end–8 sts remain. Work even for 2 rnds.

Decrease Rnd 3: *K2tog; repeat from * to end–4 sts remain. Cut yarn, leaving 8" tail. Thread tail through remaining sts, pull tight, and fasten off.

spiral seat cushion

Many years ago I found a stool with a seat cushion made out of I-cord at an antique store. Since then I've been playing around with techniques for making this type of cushion, attempting to figure out how to knit it all in one piece without having to sew I-cord together, and I'm happy to have finally worked it out. I love how modern the cushions look even though their inspiration was vintage. They fit on just about any dining chair so they make a great gift even if you don't know the precise size and shape of the recipient's seating. I finished a set of two in just under six hours.

FINISHED MEASUREMENTS
Approximately 15" diameter

YARN
Blue Sky Alpacas Bulky (50% alpaca / 50% wool; 45 yards / 100 grams): 1 hank each #1004 Polar Bear (A), #1002 Silver Mink (B), and #1003 Porcupine (C)

NEEDLES
One pair double-pointed needles (dpn) size US 13 (9 mm)

Change needle size if necessary to obtain correct gauge.

NOTIONS
Removable stitch marker

GAUGE
4 sts and 6 rows = 2" (5 cm) in Stockinette stitch (St st)

Note: Each I-Cord is approximately ⁷⁄₈" wide.

NOTE
The pattern doesn't specify when to change colors; feel free to change colors whenever you choose.

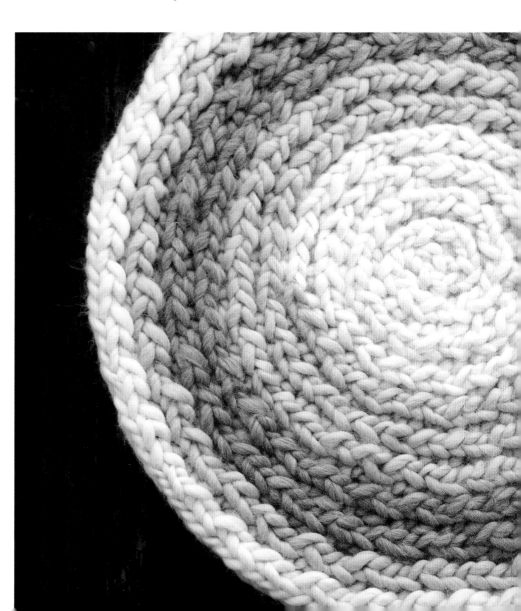

Cushion

Using A, CO 3 sts. Begin I-Cord as follows: *Transfer needle with sts to left hand, bring yarn around behind work to right-hand side; using second dpn, knit sts from right to left, pulling yarn from left to right for the first st; do not turn. Slide sts to opposite end of needle; repeat from * twice.

Begin Spiral

Rows 1-3: Slide sts to opposite end of needle, k2, slip 1 knitwise, pick up and knit 1 st in row below sts on needle, psso.

Row 4: Repeat Row 1, picking up in CO edge.

Note: This last pick-up may be tight.

Spiral Step 1

Slide sts to opposite end of needle, place removable marker through front leg of first st on needle.

Rows 1 and 2: K3; slide sts to opposite end of needle.

Row 3: K2, slip 1 knitwise, pick up and knit 1 st in row below last picked-up st, psso; slide sts to opposite end of needle.

Repeat Rows 1-3 until you come to marker.

Work Step 1 once more.

Spiral Step 2

Slide sts to opposite end of needle, remove marker and place it through front leg of first st on needle.

Rows 1, 3, and 4: K3; slide sts to opposite end of needle.

Rows 2 and 5: K2, slip 1 knitwise, pick up and knit 1 st in second row below last picked-up st, psso; slide sts to opposite end of needle.

Repeat Rows 1-5 until you come to marker.

Work Step 2 three more times.

Spiral Step 3

Slide sts to opposite end of needle, remove marker and place it through front leg of first st on needle.

Rows 1, 2, and 4-6: K3; slide sts to opposite end of needle.

Rows 3 and 7: K2, slip 1 knitwise, pick up and knit 1 st in third row below last picked-up st, psso; slide sts to opposite end of needle.

Repeat Rows 1-7 until you come to marker.

Work Step 3 three more times. *Note: Work Step 3 fewer times if your chair seat is smaller than 16" diameter.*

Next Row: K2tog, k1, pass first st over—1 st remains. Fasten off. Using tail, sew BO end to nearest point of Spiral.

To : Bear
♡ love, Joelle

To Novella
love, Joelle

easy baby cardigan

This is such an easy sweater to make, even a new knitter can take it on. I've included sizes from newborn to 9 months, but keep in mind that the larger sizes will take you longer to knit.

STITCH PATTERN
Seed Stitch (multiple of 2 sts + 1)
All Rows: K1, *p1, k1; repeat from * to end.

NOTES
The Cardigan is worked flat, but you need the length and flexibility of the circular needle to work the pattern. The Cardigan is worked in one piece from the bottom edge of the Back, over the Sleeves and shoulders, down to the bottom edge of the Fronts.

When starting a new ball of yarn, start it on the Stockinette stitch portion of the work rather than in the edge stitches; this will make weaving in the ends invisibly easier.

The pattern has two options for working the edge trim: Seed stitch as shown on the Hollyhock version or Garter stitch as shown on the Olive Leaf version. When instructions tell you to "work in trim st" over a specified length, number of rows, or number of stitches, work your preference of Seed stitch or Garter stitch (knit every row).

Back
CO 37 (39, 41) sts, leaving a 30" long tail for finishing. Begin trim st of your choice (Seed st or Garter st [knit every row]); work even for 1", ending with a WS row. Change to St st; work even until piece measures 5 (5 ½, 6)" from the beginning, ending with a WS row.

Sleeves
Next Row (RS): Using Cable CO (see page 131), CO 20 (21, 22) sts at beginning of next row; working across CO sts, work in trim st for 11 sts, pm (place marker), knit to end—57 (60, 63) sts.
Next Row: CO 20 (21, 22) sts, work in trim st for 11 sts, pm, purl to next marker, work in trim st to end—77 (81, 85) sts.
Next Row: Work in trim st to first marker, work in St st to next marker, work in trim st to end.

Work even for 2 ¼ (2 ½, 2 ¾)" if you are working Seed st trim, or for 1 ¾ (2, 2 ¼)" if you are working Garter st trim, ending with a WS row.

Shape Back Neck

Row 1 (RS): Work trim st to first marker, k14 (16, 18), pm, work in trim st over next 27 sts, pm, knit to next marker, work trim st to end.
Row 2: Work trim st to first marker, purl to next marker, work trim st to next marker, purl to last marker, work trim st to end.
Work even for 4 rows if you are working Seed st trim, or 6 rows if you are working Garter st trim.
Next Row (RS): Work to second marker, work 5 sts, BO next 17 sts for Back neck in st pattern, work to end—30 (32, 34) sts remain each side for shoulders and Sleeves.

Left Front

Working only on Left Front and Sleeve sts, and leaving remaining sts on needle, work even for 5 rows if you are working Seed st trim, or 7 rows if you are working Garter st trim.

Shape Front Neck

Row 1 (RS): Work to first marker, k1-f/b, work to end—31 (33, 35) sts.
Row 2: Work to 1 st before second marker, k1-f/b, work to end—32 (34, 36) sts.
Repeat Rows 1 and 2 five times, working increased sts in St st as they become available—42 (44, 46) sts.
Work even until piece measures 6 ½ (7, 7 ½)" from beginning of Sleeve, ending with a RS row.

Finish Sleeves

Next Row (WS): BO 20 (21, 22) sts in pattern, work to end—22 (23, 24) sts remain.
Work even for 4 (4 ½, 5)", ending with a WS row.
Next Row (RS): Change to trim st across all sts; work even for 1", ending with a WS row. BO all sts, leaving a 30" long tail for finishing.

Right Front

With WS facing, rejoin yarn to sts on needle. Work even for 5 rows if you are working Seed st trim, or 7 rows if you are working Garter st trim.

Shape Front Neck

Row 1 (RS): Work to 1 st before second marker, k1-f/b, sm, work to end—31 (33, 35) sts.
Row 2: Work to first marker, sm, k1-f/b, work to end—32 (34, 36) sts.
Repeat Rows 1 and 2 five times, working increased sts in St st as they become available—42 (44, 46) sts.
Work even until piece measures 6 ½ (7, 7 ½)" from beginning of Sleeve, ending with a WS row.

Finish Sleeves

Next Row (RS): BO 20 (21, 22) sts in pattern, work to end–22 (23, 24) sts remain.
Work even for 4 (4½, 5)", ending with a WS row.
Next Row (RS): Change to trim st across all sts; work even for 1", ending with a WS row. BO all sts, leaving a 30" long tail for finishing.

Finishing

Block if desired. Using Mattress st (see page 126) and long tails from CO and BO, sew side seams. Sew Sleeve seams. Sew buttons to Left Front for a girl, or to Right Front for a boy, with lowest button centered in edge trim, highest button ½" below end of neck shaping, and remaining 2 evenly spaced between. The buttons can be pushed through sts on the opposite Front, without stretching the sts.

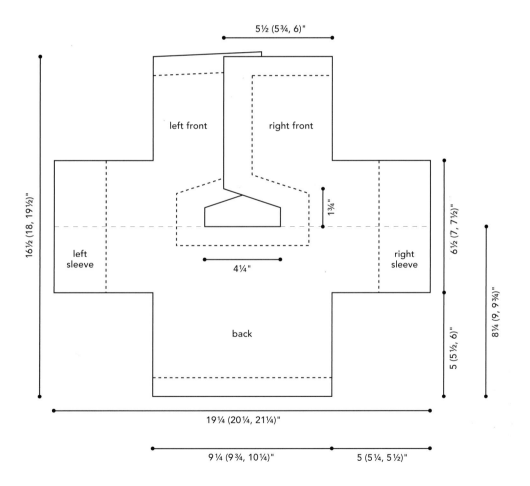

6- to 8-hour gifts

beret

I have always loved berets; they are the perfect hat for wearing indoors since they are so elegant, or outdoors to keep you warm (without squishing your hair!). This simple pattern is worked from the brim up. The decreases are not visible, freeing you to play with any color and textural changes without worrying about how they will coordinate with shaping lines. The pattern is written for two gauges, 26 stitches and 36 rounds to 4 inches, and 24 stitches and 30 rounds to 4 inches, so it will work for a lot of different yarns.

FINISHED MEASUREMENTS
18 ½" circumference, unstretched
24" circumference, stretched

NOTIONS
Stitch marker

Sport Weight

YARN
Lobster Pot Yarns 2-Ply Cashmere (100% cashmere; 400 yards / 50 grams): 1 hank Chatham Light or Drawn Butter. *Note: When working with this yarn, use 2 strands of yarn held together.*

Farmhouse Yarns Fannie's Fingering (80% merino / 20% nylon; 400 yards / 4 ounces): 1 hank Toffee

Alchemy Yarns of Transformation Haiku (60% kid mohair / 40% silk; 325 yards / 25 grams): 1 hank Michelle's Marigold worked with Hand Jive Nature's Palette Plant-Dyed Merino Fingering Yarn (100% merino wool; 185 yards / 50 grams): 1 hank Lilac. *Note: Use 1 strand of each of these yarns held together.*

NEEDLES
One 16" (40 cm) long circular (circ) needle size US 1 (2.25 mm)

One 16" (40 cm) long circular needle size US 3 (3.25 mm)

One set of five double-pointed needles (dpn) size US 3 (3.25 mm)

Change needle size if necessary to obtain correct gauge.

GAUGE
26 sts and 36 rnds = 4" (10 cm) in Stockinette stitch (St st) (knit every rnd), using larger needle

DK Weight

YARN
Joseph Galler Belangor (100% angora; 33 yards / 10 grams): 5 balls #868 Canary

ShibuiKnits Merino Worsted (100% merino wool; 191 yards / 100 grams): 1 hank Bark

Manos del Uruguay Silk Blend (70% merino wool / 30% silk; 150 yards / 50 grams): 1 hank each #3044 Briar (outside edge) and #3071 Wisteria (center)

NEEDLES
One 16" (40 cm) long circular (circ) needle size US 3 (3.25 mm)

One 16" (40 cm) long circular needle size US 5 (3.75 mm)

One set of five double-pointed needles (dpn) size US 5 (3.75 mm)

Change needle size if necessary to obtain correct gauge.

GAUGE
24 sts and 30 rnds = 4" (10 cm) in Stockinette stitch (St st) (knit every rnd), using larger needle

STITCH PATTERN
1x1 Rib (multiple of 2 sts; 1-rnd repeat)
All Rnds: *K1, p1; repeat from * to end.

NOTES
Instructions for the Sport Weight version are given first, with instructions for the DK Weight version in parentheses. When only one figure is given, it applies to both versions.

If you find it difficult to cast on stitches loosely, try using a needle 2 sizes larger than the size required for the ribbing to work the cast-on row. Remember to change back to the size required before working your first rnd.

Brim
Using smaller circ needle, CO 128 (120) sts loosely. Join for working in the rnd, being careful not to twist sts; place marker (pm) for beginning of rnd. Begin 1x1 Rib; work even until piece measures 1 ¼" from the beginning.

Crown
Sport Weight Version Only
Increase Rnd: Change to larger circ needle. K2tog, *k1-f/b, k1; repeat from * to end–190 sts.

DK Weight Version Only
Increase Rnd: Change to larger circ needle. *K1-f/b, k1; repeat from * to end–180 sts.

Both Versions
Next Rnd: Change to St st (knit every rnd); work even until piece measures 4½" from the beginning. *Note: If you prefer a more relaxed Beret, work even until piece measures 5-6" from the beginning.*

Shape Crown
Note: Change to dpns when necessary for number of sts on needle.
Decrease Rnd 1: *K3, k2tog; repeat from * to end–152 (144) sts remain. Work even for 1".
Decrease Rnd 2: *K2, k2tog; repeat from * to end–114 (108) sts remain. Work even for 1".
Decrease Rnd 3: *K1, k2tog; repeat from * to end–76 (72) sts remain. Work even for 1".
Decrease Rnd 4: *K2tog; repeat from * to end–38 (36) sts remain. Work even for ¾".
Decrease Rnd 5: *K2tog; repeat from * to end–19 (18) sts remain. Knit 1 rnd.
Decrease Rnd 6: K1 (0), *k2tog; repeat from * to end–10 (9) sts remain. Knit 1 rnd.
Decrease Rnd 7: K0 (1), *k2tog; repeat from * to end–5 (5) sts remain. Break yarn, leaving an 8" tail; thread tail through remaining sts, pull tight and fasten off, with tail to WS.

Finishing
Block as desired.

Shown clockwise from top: Manos del Uruguay Silk Blend, Joseph Galler Belangor, Alchemy Yarns of Transformation Haiku and Hand Jive Nature's Palette Plant-Dyed Merino Fingering Yarn, Farmhouse Yarns Fannie's Fingering, ShibuiKnits Merino Worsted, Lobster Pot Yarns 2-Ply Cashmere

kid's vest

SIZES
18-24 months (3-4 years, 5-6 years, 7-8 years, 9-10 years)

FINISHED MEASUREMENTS
23 ½ (26 ¼, 29 ¼, 32, 34 ¾)" chest

YARN
Spud & Chloë Sweater (55% superwash wool / 45% organic cotton; 160 yards / 100 grams): 2 (2, 2, 2, 3) hank(s) #7500 Ice Cream (size 3-4 years) or #7506 Toast (size 5-6 years for MC); small amounts #7501 Popsicle (size 3-4 years) or #7500 Ice Cream (size 5-6 years) for Duplicate Stitch

NEEDLES
One 24" (60 cm) circular (circ) needle size US 9 (5.5 mm)

One 24" (60 cm) circular needle size US 7 (4.5 mm)

One set of five double-pointed needles (dpn) size US 7 (4.5 mm)

Change needle size if necessary to obtain correct gauge.

GAUGE
17 sts and 22 rnds = 4" (10 cm) in Stockinette stitch (St st) (knit every rnd), using larger needles

NOTIONS
Stitch marker; stitch holders; water-soluble disappearing fabric marker (optional); tapestry needle

The simple shape of this classic child's vest lends itself to finishing with a personal detail, such as a first initial worked in duplicate stitch. For charts of letters and numbers, see page 134.

STITCH PATTERN
1x1 Rib (multiple of 2 sts; 1-rnd repeat)
All Rnds: *K1, p1; repeat from * to end

Body
Using smaller circ needle and MC, CO 100 (112, 124, 136, 148) sts. Join for working in the rnd, being careful not to twist sts; place marker (pm) for beginning of rnd. Begin 1x1 Rib; work even for 4 rnds.
Next Rnd: Change to larger needles and St st (knit every rnd); work even until piece measures 7 (8, 9, 10, 11)" from the beginning.

Divide for Front and Back
Row 1 (RS): K2 (4, 6, 7, 8), place last 4 (8, 12, 14, 16) sts worked on holder for underarm, k46 (48, 50, 54, 58) and place on holder for Back (or leave sts on circ while you work the Front), k4 (8, 12, 14, 16) and place on holder for underarm, knit to end.

Front

Shape Armholes
Working on Front sts only, purl 1 row.
Next Row (RS): Decrease 1 st each side this row, then every other row 4 (5, 5, 5, 6) times, as follows: Ssk, knit to last 2 sts, k2tog—36 (36, 38, 42, 44) sts remain. Work even for 2 rows.

Shape Neck
Decrease Row 1 (RS): K13 (13, 14, 16, 17), k2tog, k1, turn—15 (15, 16, 18, 19) sts remain for left shoulder.
Decrease Row 2: P1, p2tog, work to end—14 (14, 15, 17, 18) sts remain.
Decrease Row 3: Working only on left shoulder sts, knit to last 3 sts, k2tog, k1—13 (13, 14, 16, 17) sts remain.
Work Decrease Rows 2 and 3 until 8 (8, 9, 10, 11) sts remain. Work even until piece measures 12 ½ (14 ¼, 15 ¼, 16 ¼, 17 ¾)" from the beginning, ending with a RS row. Break yarn, leaving a long tail for finishing. Place sts on holder.

Shown from left to right:
Ice Cream and Toast

Note: The shoulders will be joined using Kitchener st (see page 128). If you are not comfortable with Kitchener st, you may either BO the shoulder sts now and sew the shoulder seams when finishing, or leave the sts on st holders now and join the shoulders when finishing using Three-Needle BO (see page 133). For either of the latter options, end with a WS row instead of a RS row.

Next Row (RS): With RS facing, rejoin yarn to remaining sts. K4 and place on holder for finishing, k1, ssk, knit to end—15 (15, 16, 18, 19) sts remain for right shoulder.
Decrease Row 2: Work to last 3 sts, ssp, p1—14 (14, 15, 17, 18) sts remain.
Decrease Row 3: K1, ssk, knit to end—13 (13, 14, 16, 17) sts remain.
Work Decrease Rows 2 and 3 until 8 (8, 9, 10, 11) sts remain. Work even until piece measures 12½ (14¼, 15¼, 16¼, 17¾)" from the beginning, ending with a RS row. Break yarn, leaving a long tail for finishing. Place sts on holder.

Back

Shape Armholes
With WS facing, rejoin yarn to left underarm. Purl 1 row.
Next Row (RS): Decrease 1 st each side this row, then every other row 4 (5, 5, 5, 6) times, as follows: Ssk, knit to last 2 sts, k2tog—36 (36, 38, 42, 44) sts remain. Work even until piece measures 11 (13, 14, 14¾, 16¼)", ending with a WS row.

Shape Neck
Decrease Row 1 (RS): K10 (10, 11, 13, 14), k2tog, k1, turn—12 (12, 13, 15, 16) sts remain for right shoulder.
Decrease Row 2: P1, p2tog, work to end—11 (11, 12, 14, 15) sts remain.
Decrease Row 3: Working only on right shoulder sts, knit to last 3 sts, k2tog, k1—10 (10, 11, 13, 14) sts remain.
Work Decrease Rows 2 and 3 until 8 (8, 9, 10, 11) sts remain. Work even until piece measures 12½ (14¼, 15¼, 16¼, 17¾)" from the beginning, ending with a RS row. Break yarn, leaving a long tail for finishing. Place sts on holder.
Next Row (RS): With RS facing, rejoin yarn to remaining sts. K10 and place on holder for finishing, k1, ssk, knit to end—12 (12, 13, 15, 16) sts remain for left shoulder.
Decrease Row 2: Work to last 3 sts, ssp, p1—11 (11, 12, 14, 15) sts remain.
Decrease Row 3: K1, ssk, knit to end—10 (10, 11, 13, 14) sts remain.
Work Decrease Rows 2 and 3 until 8 (8, 9, 10, 11) sts remain. Work even until piece measures 12½ (14¼, 15¼, 16¼, 17¾)" from the beginning, ending with a RS row. Break yarn, leaving a long tail for finishing. Place sts on holder.

Finishing
Using Kitchener st, graft shoulder sts. *Note: If you chose not to use Kitchener st, sew shoulder seams or join shoulder sts using Three-Needle BO.*

Armhole Edging

Using dpns and MC, k4 (8, 12, 14, 16) from holder for underarm, pick up and knit approximately 3 sts for every 4 rows around armhole edge, ending with an even number of sts. *Note: You might be tempted to pick up sts through the largish gaps left by the decreases on the shaped edge, but don't or your pick-up row will have gaps at its edge. Pick up through the tighter sts around the edges instead.* Join for working in the rnd. Begin 1x1 Rib; work even for 3 rnds. BO all sts in pattern.

Neckband

Using dpns and MC, k10 from holder for center Back neck, pick up and knit approximately 3 sts for every 4 sts or rows to center Front neck, k4 from holder for center Front neck, pick up and knit approximately 3 sts for every 4 sts or rows to center Back neck, ending with an even number of sts. Join for working in the rnd. Begin 1x1 Rib; work even for 4 rnds. BO all sts in pattern loosely. *Note: To ensure that your BO is not too tight, you might want to use a larger needle to BO so that the neck opening will fit over the wearer's head.*

Duplicate Stitch Pattern

Work your choice of letters or numbers in Duplicate st (see page 130) on front of sweater.

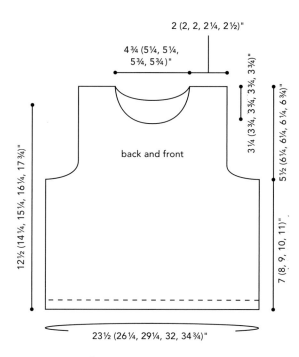

2 (2, 2, 2¼, 2½)"

4¾ (5¼, 5¼, 5¾, 5¾)"

3¼ (3¾, 3¾, 3¾, 3¾)"

5½ (6¼, 6¼, 6¼, 6¾)"

12½ (14¼, 15¼, 16¼, 17¾)"

back and front

7 (8, 9, 10, 11)"

23½ (26¼, 29¼, 32, 34¾)"

dreaming of spring fingerless gloves

PLAIN GLOVES

SIZES
Child's Medium (Child's Large/
Adult Small; Women's Medium;
Women's Large/Men's Small;
Men's Medium)

FINISHED MEASUREMENTS
6 (6 ¾, 7 ¼, 8, 8 ¾)" circumference

YARN
Alchemy Yarns of Transformation
Temple (100% superfine merino;
128 yards / 50 grams): 1 (2, 2, 2,
2) hank(s) #65E Dragon (Women's
Large/Men's Small) or #21E Green
Plum (Men's Medium)

NEEDLES
One set of four double-pointed
needles (dpn) size US 5 (3.75 mm)

One set of four double-pointed
needles size US 4 (3.5 mm)

Change needle size if necessary
to obtain correct gauge.

NOTIONS
Stitch marker; waste yarn

GAUGE
24 sts and 36 rnds = 4" (10 cm)
in Stockinette stitch (St st) (knit
every rnd), using larger needles

Fingerless gloves are a fantastic gift for people who spend a lot of time working with their hands outdoors (I love to wear them in early spring when I'm hunting in the garden for signs of life). I started out with the idea that these gloves should be unisex but then couldn't resist adding the Aran variation for women (see photo on page 80). The yarn is Alchemy's Temple, a superfine merino that comes in a rainbow of gorgeous hand-dyed colors and is machine-washable.

ABBREVIATION
M1-p-tbl: With tip of left-hand needle inserted from front to back, lift strand between 2 needles onto left-hand needle; purl strand through back loop to increase 1 st.

STITCH PATTERNS
2x2 Rib (multiple of 4 sts; 1-rnd repeat)
All Rnds: *K2, p2; repeat from * to end.

1x1 Rib (multiple of 2 sts; 1-rnd repeat)
All Rnds: *K1, p1; repeat from * to end.

Right and Left Glove (both alike)

Cuff
Using smaller needles, CO 36 (40, 44, 48, 52) sts. Divide sts among 3 needles. Join for working in the rnd, being careful not to twist sts; place marker (pm) for beginning of rnd. Begin 2x2 Rib; work even until piece measures 2 ½ (2 ¾, 3, 3, 3)" from the beginning.

Thumb Gusset
Set-Up Rnd: Change to larger needles and St st (knit every rnd). Knit to last 3 sts, pm, knit to end.
Increase Rnd: Increase 2 sts this rnd, then every 3 rnds 5 (6, 7, 7, 7) times, as follows: Work to marker, M1-r, slip marker (sm), k1, M1-l, knit to end—48 (54, 60, 64, 68) sts. Work even for 1 rnd.

Divide for Thumb: Work 34 (38, 42, 46, 50) sts, place next 12 (14, 16, 16, 16) sts on waste yarn for Thumb, removing marker, rejoin for working in the rnd, knit to end–36 (40, 44, 48, 52) sts remain.

Hand
Work even for 8 rnds.
Next Rnd: Change to smaller needles and 1x1 Rib; work even for 10 (12, 12, 12, 14) rnds. BO all sts loosely in pattern.

Thumb
Transfer sts from waste yarn to 3 of the smaller dpns. Rejoin yarn.
Rnd 1: *K1, p1; repeat from * to end, pick up and knit 2 sts from gap, as follows: M1-l, M1-p-tbl–14 (16, 18, 18, 18) sts. Work even until piece measures 1". BO all sts loosely in pattern.

Finishing
Block if desired.

CABLED FINGERLESS GLOVES

SIZES
Child's Medium (Child's Large/
Women's Small, Women's Medium,
Women's Large)

FINISHED MEASUREMENTS
6 ¼ (7, 7 ½, 8 ¼)" circumference

YARN
Alchemy Yarns of Transformation
Temple (100% superfine merino;
128 yards / 50 grams): 2 hanks
#65e Dragon

NEEDLES
One set of four double-pointed
needles (dpn) size US 5 (3.75 mm)

One set of four double-pointed
needles size US 4 (3.5 mm)

Change needle size if necessary to
obtain correct gauge.

NOTIONS
Stitch marker; cable needle (cn);
waste yarn

GAUGE
24 sts and 36 rnds = 4" (10 cm)
in Stockinette stitch (St st) (knit
every rnd), using larger needles

ABBREVIATIONS
C4F: Slip 2 sts to cn, hold to front, k2, k2 from cn.

C4B: Slip 2 sts to cn, hold to back, k2, k2 from cn.

M1-p-tbl: With tip of left-hand needle inserted from front to back, lift strand between 2 needles onto left-hand needle; purl strand through back loop to increase 1 st.

STITCH PATTERN
2x2 Rib (multiple of 4 sts; 1-rnd repeat)
All Rnds: *K2, p2; repeat from * to end.

Cable Panel (panel of 14 sts; 4-rnd repeat)
Rnd 1: K2, [C4F] 3 times.
Rnd 2: K14.
Rnd 3: [C4B] 3 times, k2.
Rnd 4: K14.
Repeat Rnds 1-4 for Cable Panel.

1x1 Rib (multiple of 2 sts; 1-rnd repeat)
All Rnds: *K1, p1; repeat from * to end.

Left Glove

Cuff
Using smaller needles, CO 36 (40, 44, 48) sts. Divide sts among 3 needles. Join for working in the rnd, being careful not to twist sts; place marker (pm) for beginning of rnd. Begin 2x2 Rib; work even until piece measures 2 ½ (2 ¾, 3, 3)" from the beginning.

Thumb Gusset
Begin Cable Panel.
Set-Up Rnd 1: Change to larger needles. K3 (4, 5, 6), p2, M1-p, [k1, k1-f/b, M1-l] 3 times, k2, M1-p, p2, knit to end—44 (48, 52, 56) sts.
Set-Up Rnd 2: K3 (4, 5, 6), p3, work Cable Panel over 14 sts, p3, knit to last 3 sts, pm, knit to end.
Increase Rnd: Increase 2 sts this rnd, then every 3 rnds 5 (6, 7, 7) times, as follows: Work to marker, M1-r, slip marker (sm), k1, M1-l, knit to end—56 (62, 68, 72) sts. Work even for 1 rnd.
Divide for Thumb: Work 42 (46, 50, 54) sts, place next 12 (14, 16, 16) sts on waste yarn for Thumb, removing marker, rejoin for working in the rnd, knit to end—44 (48, 52, 56) sts remain.

Hand

Work even for 8 rnds.

Next Rnd: Change to smaller needles. K1 (0, 1, 0), [p1, k1] 1 (2, 2, 3) times, work next 20 sts as established, *k1, p1; repeat from * to last 3 (4, 3, 4) sts, k1 (0, 1, 0), p2tog, k0 (1, 0, 1)–43 (47, 51, 55) sts remain. Work even for 11 rnds. BO all sts loosely in pattern. *Note: You may want to work a few decreases across the Cable Panel sts while binding off, so that the BO edge does not flare.*

Thumb

Transfer 12 (14, 16, 16) sts from waste yarn to 3 dpns. Rejoin yarn.

Rnd 1: *K1, p1; repeat from * to end, pick up and knit 2 sts from gap, as follows: M1-l, M1-p-tbl–14 (16, 18, 18) sts. Work even until piece measures 1". BO all sts loosely in pattern.

Right Glove

Work as for Left Glove to beginning of Thumb Gusset.

Thumb Gusset

Begin Cable Panel

Set-Up Rnd 1: Change to larger needles. K3 (4, 5, 6), p2, M1-p, [k1, k1-f/b, M1-l] 3 times, k2, M1-p, p2, knit to end–44 (48, 52, 56) sts.

Set-Up Rnd 2: K3 (4, 5, 6), p3, work Cable Panel over 14 sts, p3, k5 (6, 7, 8), pm, knit to end. Work as for Left Glove to end of Thumb Gusset.

Divide for Thumb: Work 28 (30, 32, 34) sts, place next 12 (14, 16, 16) sts on waste yarn for Thumb, removing marker, knit to end. Complete as for Left Glove.

Finishing

Block if desired.

very pretty lace scarf

FINISHED MEASUREMENTS
6" wide x 42" long, after blocking

YARN
Wagtail Yarns 100% Kid Mohair
Yarn 4-Ply (100% kid mohair; 410
yards / 100 grams): 1 hank Bronze

NEEDLES
One 16" (40 cm) long circular (circ)
needle size US 7 (4.5 mm)

Change needle size if necessary to
obtain correct gauge.

NOTIONS
Stitch marker

GAUGE
25 sts and 30 rnds = 4" (10 cm) in
Openwork Pattern, after blocking

I worked this feminine scarf in the round in a long tube to retain the springiness of the beautiful lace. If I had worked it flat and wanted to keep the edges from curling, I would have had to either block it heavily (and, in the process, lose depth and springiness) or add a substantial edge stitch, which I didn't think would look as appealing. It is made with one hank of 4-ply kid mohair from Wagtail Yarns. I find this yarn incredibly beautiful; every color is like a radiant jewel that shines and glows.

STITCH PATTERN
Openwork Pattern (multiple of 2 sts + 1; 4-rnd repeat)
Rnds 1 and 3: Knit.
Rnd 2: K1, *yo, k2tog; repeat from * to end.
Rnd 4: *Ssk, yo; repeat from * to last st, k1.
Repeat Rnds 1-4 for Openwork Pattern.

Scarf
CO 75 sts. Join for working in the rnd, being careful not to twist sts; place marker (pm) for beginning of rnd. Begin St st (knit every rnd); work even for 1". Change to Openwork Pattern; work even until piece measures 41" from the beginning, stretching slightly. Change to St st; work even for 1". BO all sts loosely.

Finishing
Block to measurements.

nesting squares
baby blanket / play mat

FINISHED MEASUREMENTS
30" square, after blocking

YARN
Lorna's Laces Shepherd Worsted
(100% superwash wool; 225 yards
/ 100 grams): 1 hank each Natural
(A), Sunshine (B), Firefly (C),
Harvest (D), and Pale Pink (E)

NEEDLES
One 60" (150 cm) long circular (circ)
needle size US 10 ½ (6.5 mm)

*Note: If you prefer, you may begin
with a shorter circ needle, then
change to the longer length when
desired to accommodate number
of sts on needle.*

Change needle size if necessary to
obtain correct gauge.

NOTIONS
Crochet hook size US J10 (6 mm);
4 stitch markers; waste yarn;
tapestry needle

GAUGE
13 sts and 20 rows = 4" (10 cm) in
Stockinette stitch (St st), using 2
strands of yarn held together.

Blankets are the perfect canvas for playing with color. This one is worked from the center out in five different colors that form a series of nesting squares. It's easy enough for a beginner to make while still being interesting enough to hold a more advanced knitter's attention. A little thicker than a typical baby blanket, it can do double-duty as a play mat.

Mat

Using Provisional (Crochet Chain) CO (see page 132) and 2 strands of A held together, CO 6 sts.

Set-Up Row (RS): *K1, place marker (pm); repeat from * to last 2 sts, k2.

Row 1 and all WS Rows: Purl.

Row 2: K1, [M1-r, slip marker (sm), k1, M1-l] 4 times, k1—14 sts.

Row 4: [Knit to marker, M1-r, sm, k1, M1-l] 4 times, knit to end—22 sts.

Repeat Rows 3 and 4, changing to 2 strands each of B, C, then D at the beginning of a row, as each hank runs out. *Note: Make sure last row worked with D is a WS row. Side seam will be sewn in segments, using color to match sides being sewn together; when changing colors, make sure to leave long enough tail to sew portion of side seam worked in that color.*

Next Row (RS): Change to E. Knit 8 rows. BO all sts loosely knitwise.

Finishing

Using Mattress st (see page 126) and tails left when changing colors, sew seam, beginning from outer edge and working in to center. Carefully unpick Provisional CO; thread tail from first A row through live sts, pull tight, and fasten off. Block piece to measurements.

cozy, comfy pullover

SIZES
Child's 2 (Child's 4, Child's 6, Child's 8, Child's 10, Child's 12, Women's Small, Women's Medium, Women's Large/Men's Small, Women's 1X-Large/Men's Medium, Women's 2X-Large/Men's Large)

FINISHED MEASUREMENTS
21 (23, 25, 27, 29, 31, 34, 38, 42, 46, 50)" chest

YARN
Spud & Chloë Outer (65% superwash wool / 35% organic cotton; 60 yards / 100 grams): 5 (6, 7, 8, 9, 10, 12, 13, 15, 16, 17) hanks #7200 Soapstone

NEEDLES
Two 24" (60 cm) long (or longer for larger sizes) circular (circ) needles size US 13 (9 mm)

One 16" (40 cm) long circular needle size US 13 (9 mm)

One set of five double-pointed needles (dpn) size US 13 (9 mm)

One 16" (40 cm) long circular needle size US 11 (8 mm)

Change needle size if necessary to obtain correct gauge.

NOTIONS
Removable stitch markers (including 1 in contrasting color); stitch holders; waste yarn

GAUGE
10 sts and 14 rnds = 4" (10 cm) in Stockinette stitch (St st) (knit every rnd), using larger needle

This is such a classic that I've sized it from a child's size 2 to a men's large. Child's sizes 2-6 can be completed in less than 8 hours, but the larger sizes will take longer.

Body
Using 24" long or longer circ needle, CO 27 (29, 32, 34, 37, 39, 43, 48, 53, 58, 63) sts, place marker (pm) for left side, CO 27 (29, 32, 34, 37, 39, 43, 48, 53, 58, 63) sts—54 (58, 64, 68, 74, 78, 86, 96, 106, 116, 126) sts. Join for working in the rnd, being careful not to twist sts; pm for beginning of rnd. Begin St st (knit every rnd); work even until piece measures 10 (10¾, 11½, 12¼, 13¾, 14¾, 17, 16¼, 17½, 17½, 16½)", or to desired length from the beginning, with CO edge unrolled, ending last rnd 1 (2, 2, 2, 2, 2, 2, 3, 3, 4, 5) sts past beginning of rnd marker. Place last 2 (4, 4, 4, 4, 4, 4, 6, 6, 8, 10) sts worked on holder for underarm, removing marker. Work to 1 (2, 2, 2, 2, 2, 2, 3, 3, 4, 5) sts past next marker, place last 2 (4, 4, 4, 4, 4, 4, 6, 6, 8, 10) sts worked on holder for underarm, removing marker—25 (25, 28, 30, 33, 35, 39, 42, 47, 50, 53) sts remain each for Front and Back. Leave sts on needle; set aside.

Sleeves
Using dpns, CO 18 (20, 20, 24, 24, 24, 26, 26, 28, 28, 28) sts. Divide sts among 4 needles. Join for working in the rnd, being careful not to twist sts; use the gap between the needles and the tail from the CO to keep track of the beginning of rnd. Begin St st; work even until piece measures 4" from the beginning, with CO edge unrolled.

Shape Sleeve
Increase Rnd: Increase 2 sts this rnd, then every 5 (10, 8, 27, 15, 12, 21, 11, 9, 8, 6) rnds 3 (2, 3, 1, 2, 3, 2, 4, 5, 6, 8) times, as follows: K1-f/b, knit to last st, k1-f/b—26 (26, 28, 28, 30, 32, 32, 36, 40, 42, 46) sts. Work even until piece measures 10½ (12½, 13½, 14½, 15½, 17, 19, 20, 20½, 21½, 22)", or to desired length from the beginning, with CO edge unrolled, ending 1 (2, 2, 2, 2, 2, 2, 3, 3, 4, 5) sts past beginning of rnd. Place last 2 (4, 4, 4, 4, 4, 4, 6, 6, 8, 10) sts worked on holder for underarm. Transfer remaining 24 (22, 24, 24, 26, 28, 28, 30, 34, 34, 36) sts to waste yarn for Left Sleeve. Set aside. Repeat for Right Sleeve but leave sts on needle.

Yoke

Join Body and Sleeves
Continuing in St st, and working sts onto needle holding Front and Back, pm

of different color for beginning of rnd, work across 24 (22, 24, 24, 26, 28, 28, 30, 34, 34, 36) sts for Right Sleeve, pm, work across 25 (25, 28, 30, 33, 35, 39, 42, 47, 50, 53) sts for Back, pm, work across 24 (22, 24, 24, 26, 28, 28, 30, 34, 34, 36) sts for Left Sleeve from waste yarn, pm, work across to last 2 sts of Front.

Shape Underarm

Decrease Rnd 1: Decrease 4 sts this rnd, then every other rnd 0 (0, 0, 0, 1, 1, 1, 1, 2, 3, 4) times, as follows, ending final repeat 1 st before beginning of rnd marker: [K2tog, slip marker (sm), knit to next marker, sm, ssk, knit to 2 sts before next marker] twice—94 (90, 100, 104, 110, 118, 126, 136, 150, 152, 158) sts remain. Reposition markers as follows: Move first (beginning of rnd) and third markers 1 st to the right, and second and fourth markers 1 st to the left.

Shape Sleeve Cap

Decrease Rnd 2: Decrease 4 sts this rnd, then every other rnd 3 (6, 6, 7, 5, 4, 6, 6, 4, 5, 6) times, then every rnd 4 (0, 1, 0, 3, 5, 3, 4, 8, 7, 7) times, as follows, ending final repeat 1 st before beginning of rnd marker: [sm, ssk, knit to 2 sts before next marker, k2tog, sm, knit to next marker] twice—62 (62, 68, 72, 74, 78, 86, 92, 98, 100, 102) sts remain [8 sts each Sleeve; 23 (23, 26, 28, 29, 31, 35, 38, 41, 42, 43) sts each Front and Back]. Reposition markers as follows: Move first (beginning of rnd) and third markers 1 st to the left, and second and fourth markers 1 st to the right. *Note: Change to 16" circ needle when necessary for number of sts on needle.*

Shape Shoulders

Repeat Decrease Rnd 1 this rnd, then every rnd 3 (3, 4, 4, 4, 5, 6, 7, 9, 9, 9) times, ending final repeat 2 sts before end of rnd–46 (46, 48, 52, 54, 54, 58, 60, 58, 60, 62) sts remain.

Shape Shoulders and Back Neck

Note: Back Neck is shaped using short rows (see page 132).

Rows 1 and 2: K2tog, sm, knit to next marker, sm, ssk, knit to 3 sts before next marker, wrp-t, purl to 3 sts before next marker, wrp-t.

Next Rnd: Working wrap together with wrapped st as you come to it, knit to 2 sts before third marker, k2tog, sm, knit to next marker, sm, ssk, knit to end–42 (42, 44, 48, 50, 50, 54, 56, 54, 56, 58) sts remain. Work even for 1 rnd, working remaining wrap together with wrapped st as you come to it, and removing all but beginning of rnd marker.

Next Rnd: Change to smaller circ needle. Work even for 10 (10, 10, 11, 11, 11, 12, 12, 13, 13, 13) rnds. Change to larger 16" circ needle. Work even for 1 rnd. BO all sts loosely. *Note: If your BO is too tight, consider using a needle 1 or 2 sizes larger for working BO.*

Finishing

Using Kitchener st (see page 128), graft underarm sts. Block if desired.

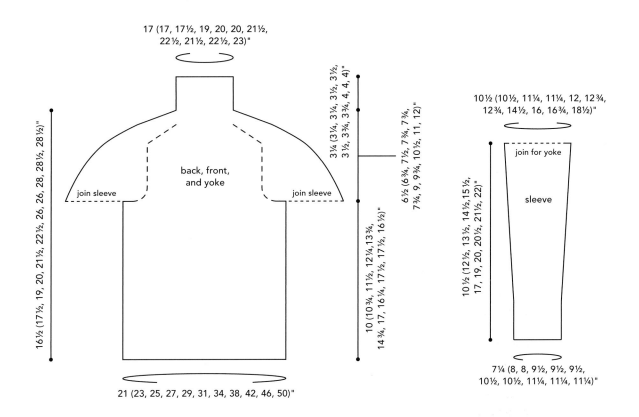

17 (17, 17½, 19, 20, 20, 21½, 22½, 21½, 22½, 23)"

3¼ (3¼, 3¼, 3¼, 3½, 3½, 3¾, 4, 4, 4)"

6½ (6¾, 7½, 7¾, 7¾, 7¾, 9, 9¾, 10½, 11, 12)"

10 (10¾, 11½, 12¼, 13¾, 14¾, 17, 16¼, 17½, 17½, 16½)"

16½ (17½, 19, 20, 21½, 22½, 26, 26, 28, 28½)"

join sleeve

back, front, and yoke

join sleeve

21 (23, 25, 27, 29, 31, 34, 38, 42, 46, 50)"

10½ (10½, 11¼, 11¼, 12, 12¾, 12¾, 14½, 16, 16¾, 18½)"

join for yoke

sleeve

10½ (12½, 13½, 14½, 15½, 17, 19, 20, 20½, 21½, 22)"

7¼ (8, 8, 9½, 9½, 9½, 10½, 10½, 11¼, 11¼, 11¼)"

more-than-8-hour gifts

entrelac baby blanket

FINISHED MEASUREMENTS
Approximately 32" square

YARN
Lobster Pot Yarns Bulky Cashmere (100% cashmere; 70 yards / 50 grams): 170 yards Sea Lettuce (A); 45 yards Sea Grass (B)

Jade Sapphire 100% Mongolian Cashmere 12 Ply (100% Mongolian cashmere; 60 yards / 55 grams): 130 yards Tweety (C); 170 yards each Jasmine (D) and Ivory (E)

Note: If you would like to substitute another yarn for the yarn used here, choose a yarn with a Stockinette stitch (St st) gauge of 12-14 sts = 4" (10 cm).

NEEDLES
One 36" (90 cm) long circular (circ) needle size US 10 ½ (6.5 cm)

Change needle size if necessary to obtain correct gauge.

GAUGE
14 sts and 28 rows = 4" (10 cm) in Garter stitch (knit every row)

The interlocking diamond shapes on this cheerful blanket are made using the entrelac technique, which means there's no sewing required. I chose a bulky yarn for this project, but it can be easily adapted to any yarn weight. If you change the weight of the yarn, of course the size of the blanket will change as well, unless you adjust the number of stitches you cast on. As you decide what you want to do, remember that the number of stitches you cast on must be divisible by the number of triangles you want at the base. For example, in the blanket shown, the cast-on number is divisible by two because there are two triangles at the bottom edge. If you want to make a blanket with three triangles, you need to cast on a number of stitches divisible by three, and so on.

Blanket
Using A, CO 72 sts.

TIER 1 (2 Triangles)

Bottom Left Triangle
Row 1 (WS): K1, turn.
Note: Since this Blanket is worked in Garter st (knit every row), you might want to place a removable marker on the second row to indicate RS.
Row 2: Knit to end.
Row 3: K2, turn.
Row 4: Knit to end.
Row 5: K3, turn.
Row 6: Knit to end.
Continue in this manner, working 1 additional st from CO edge on each WS row until you have worked 36 sts, ending on WS row; do not turn.

Bottom Right Triangle
Change to C. Work as for Bottom Left Triangle, knitting to end of color C sts on all even-numbered rows; do not work across color A sts from Bottom Left Triangle. Turn after last row, but do not knit to end.

TIER 2 (Triangle, Square, Triangle)

Right Triangle

Change to D.

Row 1 (RS): K1, turn.

Row 2: K1-f/b, turn.

Row 3: K1, ssk (1 st from current Triangle together with 1 st on left-hand needle from previous Tier), turn.

Row 4: K1-f/b, k1, turn.

Row 5: Knit to last st in D, ssk, turn.

Row 6: Knit to last 2 sts, k1-f/b, k1, turn.

Repeat Rows 5 and 6 until all 36 sts in C on left-hand needle from previous Tier have been worked, ending with a RS row; do not turn.

Square

Change to E.

Row 1 (RS): Pick up and knit 36 sts along left edge of Bottom Right Triangle, turn.

Row 2: K36, turn.

Row 3: Knit to last st in E, ssk (1 st from current Square together with 1 st on left-hand needle from previous Tier), turn.

Repeat Rows 2 and 3 until all 36 sts in A on left-hand needle from previous Tier have been worked, ending with a RS row; do not turn.

Left Triangle

Continue with E.

Row 1 (RS): Pick up and knit 36 sts along right edge of Bottom Left Triangle, turn.

Row 2: K36, turn.

Row 3: Knit to last 2 sts, k2tog, turn.

Row 4: Knit to end of triangle, turn.

Repeat Rows 3 and 4 until 1 st remains, ending with Row 3; turn after last row, but do not knit to end.

TIER 3 (2 Squares)

Left Square

Change to C.

Row 1 (WS): P1, pick up and purl 35 sts along right side edge of Tier 2 Left Triangle, turn.

Work as for Tier 2 Square, beginning with Row 2, and ending with a WS row, do not turn.

Right Square

Change to A.

Row 1 (WS): Pick up and purl 36 sts along right side edge of Tier 2 Square, turn.

Work as for Tier 2 Square, beginning with Row 2, and ending with a WS row, turn.

TIER 4 (Triangle, Square, Triangle)

Work as for Tier 2, working Right Triangle with E, Square with D, and Left Triangle with D.

TIER 5

Top Left Triangle

Change to A.

Row 1 (WS): P1, pick up and purl 36 sts along right side edge of Tier 4 Left Triangle, turn.

Row 2: Knit to last 2 sts, k2tog, turn.

Row 3: Knit to last st in A, ssk (1 st from current Triangle together with 1 st on left-hand needle from previous Tier), turn.

Repeat Rows 2 and 3 until 1 st remains, ending with Row 3; do not turn.

Top Right Triangle

Change to B.

Row 1 (WS): Slip st from right-hand needle to left-hand needle, p1, pick up and purl 36 sts along edge of Tier 4 Square, turn.

Work as for Top Left Triangle, beginning with Row 2. Fasten off.

Finishing

Block as desired.

soft as a cloud cowls

There is nothing quite like wearing a super-soft cowl of cashmere around your neck. These are made with Jade Sapphire's 2-ply cashmere, a delicate and incredibly soft yarn that is so lightweight it almost floats! I've always been amazed by the stitch definition you can achieve with this yarn and so I've provided three lovely and delicate stitch-pattern options to show it off. Each cowl takes less than one hank of yarn and makes a gorgeous, special gift.

FINISHED MEASUREMENTS
Open Mock Cable Rib:
20" circumference x 12" high

Spiral Rib:
20¼" circumference x 12" high

*Open Mock Cable
and Spiral Rib:*
20 ¾" circumference x 12" high

YARN
Jade Sapphire Mongolian Cashmere 2-ply (100% Mongolian cashmere; 400 yards / 55 grams): 1 hank each Hibiscus (Open Mock Cable Rib), Mulberry (Spiral Rib), or Peach Honey (Open Mock Cable and Spiral Rib)

NEEDLES
One 16" (40 cm) long circular (circ) needle size US 4 (3.5 mm)

Change needle size if necessary to obtain correct gauge.

NOTIONS
Stitch marker

GAUGE
32 sts and 40 rnds = 4" (10 cm) in pattern stitch (all three versions are the same gauge)

ABBREVIATION
RT: K2tog, but do not drop sts from left-hand needle, insert right-hand needle between 2 sts just worked and knit first st again, slip both sts from left-hand needle together.

Shown from top to bottom:
Open Mock Cable Rib in Hibiscus,
Spiral Rib in Mulberry, and
Open Mock Cable and Spiral
Rib in Peach Honey

OPEN MOCK CABLE RIB COWL

Note: This st pattern is a multiple of 5 sts.

CO 160 sts. Join for working in the rnd, being careful not to twist sts; place marker for beginning of rnd.

Rnds 1 and 2: *K3, p2; repeat from * to end.

Rnd 3: *Slip 1, k2, psso, p2; repeat from * to end—1 st decreased each repeat.

Rnd 4: *K1, yo, k1, p2; repeat from * to end—1 st increased each repeat.

Repeat Rnds 1-4 until piece measures 12", or to desired length, ending with Rnd 1, 2, or 4. BO all sts loosely, working Rnd 1.

Finishing

Block as desired.

SPIRAL RIB COWL

Note: This st pattern is a multiple of 6 sts.

CO 162 sts. Join for working in the rnd, being careful not to twist sts; place marker for beginning of rnd.

Rnds 1 and 3: *K4, p2; repeat from * to end.

Rnd 2: *[RT] twice; p2; repeat from * to end.

Rnd 4: *K1, RT, k1, p2; repeat from * to end.

Repeat Rnds 1-4 until piece measures 12", or to desired length. BO all sts loosely, working Rnd 1.

Finishing

Block as desired.

OPEN MOCK CABLE AND SPIRAL RIB COWL

Note: This st pattern is a multiple of 11 sts.

CO 165 sts. Join for working in the rnd, being careful not to twist sts; place marker for beginning of rnd.

Rnd 1: *K3, p2, k4, p2; repeat from * to end.

Rnd 2: *K3, p2, [RT] twice, p2; repeat from * to end.

Rnd 3: *Slip 1, k2, psso, p2, k4, p2; repeat from * to end—1 st decreased each repeat.

Rnd 4: *K1, yo, k1, p2, k1, RT, k1, p2; repeat from * to end—1 st increased each repeat.

Repeat Rnds 1-4 until piece measures 12", or to desired length, ending with Rnd 1, 2, or 4. BO all sts loosely, working Rnd 1.

Finishing

Block as desired.

men's zip-up vest

SIZES
Men's Small (Medium, Large, 1X-Large)

FINISHED MEASUREMENTS
42 (45 ½, 48 ¾, 52 ¼)" chest

YARN
Blue Sky Alpacas Worsted Hand Dyes (50% alpaca / 50% merino; 100 yards / 100 grams): 7 (7, 8, 8) hanks # 2016 Chocolate

NEEDLES
One 32" (80 cm) long circular (circ) needle size US 10 ½ (6.5 mm)

One 16" (40 cm) long circular needle size US 9 (5.5 mm)

Change needle size if necessary to obtain correct gauge.

NOTIONS
Stitch holders; stitch marker; sewing needle and thread to match yarn; 25 (25, 26, 27)" molded plastic separating zipper

GAUGE
14 sts and 20 rows = 4" (10 cm) in Stockinette stitch (St st), using larger needle

Knitting sweaters for men can be challenging. A lot of designs feel too fussy for them, and even with the right design, they take forever to finish on account of their size! In my first book, I made a men's zip-front raglan, long-sleeved sweater that a lot of men seemed to appreciate, so I played it safe here and stuck with that winning theme—just took away the sleeves. Not having to knit sleeves is a great timesaver and also saves you the worry of getting the width and length right. I loved working the seeded rib stitch on the bottom border and neck; it pulls in, but not too much, and even though you have to work it slightly differently on the right and wrong sides, it ends up looking the same on both sides, which is an interesting brain tease.

STITCH PATTERN
Seeded Rib (multiple of 6 sts + 3; 2-row repeat)

Row 1 (RS): K3, *p3, k3; repeat from * to end.
Row 2: K1, *p1, k1; repeat from * to end.
Repeat Rows 1 and 2 for Seeded Rib.

1x1 Rib (multiple of 2 sts; 1-rnd repeat)
All Rnds: *K1, p1; repeat from * to end.

Body
Using larger needle, CO 147 (159, 171, 183) sts. Begin Seeded Rib; work even until piece measures 3" from the beginning, ending with a WS row.
Next Row (RS): Work 4 sts in Seeded Rib, work in St st, beginning with a knit row, to last 4 sts, work in Seeded Rib to end. Work even until piece measures 15½ (15½, 16, 16)" from the beginning, ending with a WS row.

Divide Fronts and Back
Next Row (RS): Work 41 (46, 50, 54) sts, place last 8 (12, 14, 16) sts worked on st holder for underarm, work 73 (79, 85, 91) sts, place last 8 (12, 14, 16) sts worked on st holder for underarm, work to end.

Left Front

Next Row (WS): Work 33 (34, 36, 38) sts, leaving remaining sts on needle.

Shape Armhole

Next Row (RS): Working only on Left Front sts, decrease 1 st this row, then every other row 5 (5, 6, 7) times, as follows: Ssk, work to end–27 (28, 29, 30) sts remain. Work even until armhole measures 6½ (6½, 7, 8)", ending with a RS row.

Shape Neck

Row 1 (RS): Knit to last 6 sts, k2tog, work to end–26 (27, 28, 29) sts remain.
Row 2: Work 4 sts and place on holder, p2tog, work to end–21 (22, 23, 24) sts remain.
Row 3: Knit to last 2 sts, k2tog–20 (21, 22, 23) sts remain.
Row 4: P2tog, work to end–19 (20, 21, 22) sts remain.
Repeat Rows 3 and 4 twice–15 (16, 17, 18) sts remain. Work even until armhole measures 9½ (9½, 10, 11)", ending with a RS row. Break yarn, leaving a long tail for finishing; place sts on holder. *Note: The shoulders will be joined using Kitchener st (see page 128). If you are not comfortable with Kitchener st, you may either BO the shoulder sts now and sew the shoulder seams when finishing, or leave the sts on st holders now and join the shoulders when finishing using Three-Needle BO (see page 133). For either of the latter options, end with a WS row instead of a RS row.*

Back

With WS facing, rejoin yarn to 65 (67, 71, 75) Back sts. Purl 1 row.

Shape Armhole

Next Row (RS): Decrease 1 st each side this row, then every other row 5 (5, 6, 7) times, as follows: Ssk, knit to last 2 sts, k2tog–53 (55, 57, 59) sts remain. Work even until armhole measures 9 (9, 9½, 10½)", ending with a WS row.

Shape Neck

Next Row (RS): K14 (15, 16, 17), k2tog, turn, purl to end. Place remaining 15 (16, 17, 18) sts on holder. Break yarn.
Next Row (RS): Place next 21 sts on holder for Collar. Rejoin yarn, ssk, knit to end. Purl 1 row. Place remaining 15 (16, 17, 18) sts on holder. Break yarn.

Right Front

With WS facing, rejoin yarn to Right Front sts. Work as for Left Front, reversing st patterns and shaping.

Finishing

Using Kitchener st, graft shoulder sts. *Note: If you choose not to use Kitchener st, sew shoulder seams or join shoulder sts using Three-Needle BO.*

Collar

With RS facing, using larger circ needle, work across 4 sts from Right Front neck holder, pick up and knit 17 sts along Right Front neck edge, knit across 21 sts from holder for Back neck, pick up and knit 17 sts along Left Front neck edge, work across 4 sts from Left Front neck holder— 63 sts. Work in Seeded Rib across all sts, beginning with Row 2 of pattern. Work even until piece measures 3" from pick-up row, ending with a WS row. Purl 1 row (turning row). Begin Seeded Rib, beginning with Row 1; work even until piece measures 3" from turning row. *Note: St pattern is reversed at the turning row so that when Collar is folded over at the turning row and sewn down, the Collar looks the same on both sides.* Break yarn, leaving a long tail.

Armhole Edging

Using smaller needle, knit across last 4 (6, 7, 8) sts on holder for underarm, pick up and knit approximately 3 sts for every 4 rows around armhole edge, knit across remaining 4 (6, 7, 8) sts on holder for underarm, ending with an even number of sts. Join for working in the rnd; pm for beginning of rnd. Begin 1x1 Rib; work even for 1". BO all sts in pattern.

With sewing needle and thread, beginning at turning row of Collar, sew in zipper, sewing zipper to front of Collar first, then to back of Collar, making sure sts do not show on front of Collar. Fold Collar to WS at turning row; sew BO edge of collar to pick-up row.

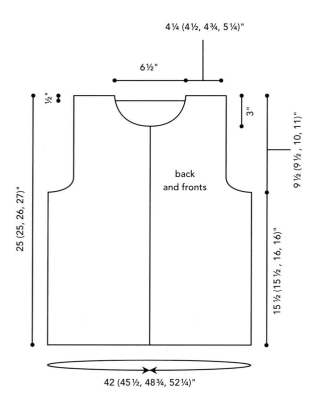

toe-up socks

These socks are the work of Leah Mitchell, a longtime Purl employee and friend (she also created Leah's Lovely Cardigan on page 111). Leah always pays careful attention to details and these socks are no exception. Each part is thoughtfully crafted, from the beautiful toe, which is virtually seamless with a lovely yarnover increase for shaping, to the sturdy heel, to the elegant rib stitch patterns that grip the foot and leg so comfortably, to the incredibly soft and beautiful yarn. They take a long time to finish, but because they are worked from the toe up, you can adapt the length to match the amount of time you can devote to them by working the first sock in a little less than half the time you have available, then finishing the second sock and sewing in your ends in the remaining time. The women's version includes a tiny mock cable that gives them a feminine touch while the men's is a double rib that is both practical and masculine.

SIZES
Note: This pattern includes instructions for both a Women's and a Men's Version. The first set of figures is for the Women's Version; the second set of figures, shown between < >, is for the Men's Version. Where there is only one set of figures, it applies to both versions.

Women's Small (Medium, Large) <Men's Small (Medium, Large)>

FINISHED MEASUREMENTS
7 (8, 9) <8 (9, 10)>" foot circumference

8 ½ (9 ½, 10 ½) <9 ½ (10 ½, 11 ½)>" foot length from Toe to back of Heel

YARN
Blue Sky Alpacas Royal (100% royal alpaca; 288 yards / 100 grams): 1 (2, 2) <2> hank(s) #700 Alabaster <#703 Cafe au Lait>

NEEDLES
One set of four double-pointed needles (dpn) size US 1 (2.25 mm)

Change needle size if necessary to obtain correct gauge.

NOTIONS
Crochet hook size US B1 (2.25 mm); stitch marker; waste yarn

GAUGE
34 sts and 40 rnds = 4" (10 cm) in Stockinette stitch (St st) (knit every rnd)

ABBREVIATION
RT: K2tog, but do not drop sts from left-hand needle, insert right-hand needle between 2 sts just worked and knit first st again, slip both sts from left-hand needle together.

STITCH PATTERNS

Twisted Rib for Foot (Women's Version only) (panel of 30 (34, 38) sts; 4-rnd repeat)

Rnds 1-3: P0 (2, 0), *k2, p2; repeat from * to last 2 (0, 2) sts, k2 (0, 2).

Rnd 4: P0 (2, 0), k0 (0, 2), p0 (0, 2), *[k2, p2] twice, RT, p2; repeat from * once, [k2, p2] 1 (2, 2) times, k2 (0, 2).

Repeat Rnds 1-4 for Twisted Rib for Foot.

Twisted Rib for Leg (Women's Version only) (multiple of 12 sts; 4-rnd repeat)

Rnds 1-3: *K2, p2; repeat from * to end.

Rnd 4: *[K2, p2] twice, RT, p2; repeat from * to end.

Repeat Rnds 1-4 for Twisted Rib for Leg.

2x2 Rib for Foot (Men's Version only) (multiple of 4 sts + 2; 1-rnd repeat)

All Rnds: K2, *p2, k2; repeat from * to end.

2x2 Rib for Leg (Men's Version only) (multiple of 4 sts; 1-rnd repeat)

All Rnds: *K2, p2; repeat from * to end.

Toe

Note: Sock is worked from the Toe up.

Using Provisional CO (see page 132), CO 8 <12> sts, leaving a long tail for finishing. Turn, k4 <6> onto Needle 1, k2 <3> each onto Needles 2 and 3. Join for working in the rnd, being careful not to twist sts; place marker (pm) for beginning of rnd. Begin St st (knit every rnd) as follows:

Shape Toe

Increase Rnd: Needle 1: K1, yo, knit to last st, yo, k1; Needle 2: K1, yo, knit to end of needle; Needle 3: Knit to last st, yo, k1–12 <16> sts.

Repeat Increase Rnd every rnd 4 (8, 12) <5 (9, 13)> times, then every other rnd 8 (6, 4) times, knitting all yo's through back loop to close the hole—60 (68, 76) <68 (76, 84)> sts [30-15-15 (34-17-17, 38-19-19) <34-17-17 (38-19-19, 42-21-21)> sts]. Work even for 6 <10> rnds.

Foot

Next Rnd: Needle 1: Work Twisted Rib for Foot <2x2 Rib for Foot>; Needles 2 and 3: Knit. Work even until piece measures 6 (6¾, 7½) <6¾ (7½, 8¼)>", or to 2½ (2¾, 3) <2¾ (3, 3¼)>" less than desired length from Toe to back of Heel.

Gusset

Rnd 1: Needle 1: Work Twisted Rib for Foot <2x2 Rib for Foot> as established; Needle 2: K1, yo, knit to end; Needle 3: Knit to last st, yo, k1–62 (70, 78) <70 (78, 86)> sts.

Rnd 2: Needle 1: Work even; Needles 2 and 3: Knit, working all yo's through back loop to close the hole.

Repeat Rnds 1 and 2 eight <9> times—78 (86, 94) <88 (96, 104)> sts [30-24-24 (34-26-26, 38-28-28) <34-27-27 (38-29-29, 42-31-31)> sts]. Work across Needle 1.

Turn Heel

Note: Heel is shaped using Short Rows (see page 132). Work all yo's through back loop as you come to them.
Row 1 (RS): Working only on Needles 2 and 3, Needle 2: Knit; Needle 3: K7 (9, 11) <8 (10, 12)>, yo, k1, wrp-t.
Row 2: P16 (20, 24) <18 (22, 26)>, yo, p1, wrp-t.
Row 3: K14 (18, 22) <16 (20, 24)>, yo, k1, wrp-t.
Row 4: P12 (16, 20) <14 (18, 22)>, yo, p1, wrp-t.
Continue to work as established, working 2 fewer sts on each row before working the yo, until you have 2 <4> sts between center yo's—56 (62, 68) <62 (68, 74)> sts on Needles 2 and 3. Work to end of Needle 3, working wraps together with wrapped sts as you come to them, work across Needle 1, then across Needle 2, working wraps together with wrapped sts as you come to them—86 (96, 106) <96 (106, 116)> sts [30-28-28 (34-31-31, 38-34-34) <34-31-31 (38-34-34, 42-37-37)> sts]. *Note: For Women's Version, make note of Rnd of Twisted Rib for Foot on which you end.*

Heel Flap

Set-Up Row 1 (RS): Needle 3: K14 (18, 16) <16 (18, 20)>, ssk, turn.
Row 1: Working only on sts on Needles 2 and 3, slip 1, p28 (36, 32) <32 (36, 40)>, p2tog, turn.
Row 2: *Slip 1, k1; repeat from * to 1 st before gap, ssk (the 2 sts on either side of gap), turn.
Row 3: Slip 1, purl to 1 st before gap, p2tog (the 2 sts on either side of gap), turn.
Repeat Rows 2 and 3 eleven (10, 15) <12 (13, 14)> times—30 (38, 34) <34 (38, 42)> sts remain.
Row 4: Needle 2: *Slip 1, k1; repeat from * to last st on needle, slip last st to Needle 3; Needle 3: *Slip 1, k1; repeat from * to end. Rejoin for working in the rnd; k0 (0, 2) <0>, p0 (2, 2) <0>, pm for beginning of rnd—60 (72, 72) <68 (76, 84)> sts [30-15-15 (38-17-17, 34-19-19) <34-17-17 (38-19-19, 42-21-21)> sts].

Leg

Next Rnd: Change to Twisted Rib for Leg <2x2 Rib for Leg> across all sts, beginning with the rnd following the rnd on which you ended before working the Heel Flap. Work even until Cuff measures 8 (8½, 9) <9 (9½, 10)>" from beginning of Heel Flap, or to desired length. BO all sts in pattern.

Finishing

Carefully unpick waste yarn and place Toe sts on 2 needles. Using Kitchener st (see page 128), graft Toe sts together. Block as desired.

leah's lovely cardigan

SIZES
Women's X-Small (Small, Medium, Large, 1X-Large, 2X-Large)

FINISHED MEASUREMENTS
30 (34 ¼, 38, 42, 45 ¾, 50)" bust, buttoned

YARN
Koigu Wool Designs Koigu Premium Merino (KPM) (100% merino wool; 175 yards / 50 grams): 8 (8, 9, 10, 11, 12) hanks #2390.5

NEEDLES
One 24" (60 cm) long or longer circular (circ) needle size US 3 (3.25 mm)

One 24" (60 cm) long or longer circular needle size US 1 (2.25 mm)

One 12" (30 cm) long circular needle size US 3 (3.25 mm)

One set of five double-pointed needles (dpn) size US 3 (3.25 mm)

One set of five double-pointed needles size US 1 (2.25 mm)

Change needle size if necessary to obtain correct gauge.

NOTIONS
Stitch markers; stitch holders; nine ³/₈" buttons

GAUGE
29 sts and 38 rows = 4" (10 cm) in Stockinette stitch (St st), using larger needles

This elegant cardigan is an original creation of Leah Mitchell, a very talented designer and friend who also designed the gorgeous socks on page 107. Leah created this sweater for herself, and as soon as I saw it I fell in love with it. Although it takes more time to knit than many of the other projects in this book, it does include some timesaving features: It is worked in one piece, so requires no sewing at the end, it has three-quarter-length sleeves, which are, obviously, quicker to knit than full-length sleeves, and the shoulder decreases are spread out evenly so you don't have to fuss with stitch markers to remember when to work them.

STITCH PATTERNS
2x1 Rib (multiple of 3 sts + 4; 1-row repeat)
Row 1 (RS): K3, *p1, k2; repeat from * to last st, k1.
Row 2: Knit the knit sts and purl the purl sts as they face you.
Repeat Row 2 for 2x1 Rib.

2x1 Rib in-the-Rnd (multiple of 3 sts)
All Rnds: *K2, p1; repeat from * to end.

Body
Using smaller 24" circ needle, CO 211 (241, 268, 298, 325, 355) sts. Begin 2x1 Rib; work even until piece measures 2" from the beginning, ending with a WS row.
Next Row (RS): Change to larger 24" circ needle and St st, beginning with a knit row; place markers (pm) 52 (60, 67, 74, 81, 89) sts in from each end. Work even until piece measures 3" from the beginning, ending with a WS row.

Shape Waist
Decrease Row (RS): Decrease 4 sts this row, then every 2" twice, as follows: Knit to 2 sts before first marker, ssk, slip marker (sm), k1, k2tog, knit to 3 sts before next marker, ssk, k1, sm, k2tog, knit to end—199 (229, 256, 286, 313, 343) sts remain. Work even for 1".

Increase Row (RS): Increase 4 sts this row, then every 2" twice, as follows: Knit to first marker, M1, sm, k1, M1, knit to 1 st before next marker, M1, k1, sm, M1, knit to end–211 (241, 268, 298, 325, 355) sts. Work even until piece measures 16¾ (16¾, 16½, 16¾, 16½, 16¾)" from the beginning, ending with a RS row.

Divide Fronts and Back

Next Row (WS): [Purl to 4 (8, 12, 16, 20, 24) sts after marker, place last 8 (16, 24, 32, 40, 48) sts worked on holder for underarm, removing markers] twice, purl to end–48 (52, 55, 58, 61, 65) sts remain each Front; 99 (105, 110, 118, 123, 129) sts remain for Back.
Set aside; do not break yarn.

Sleeves

Using smaller dpns, CO 69 (69, 72, 72, 78, 78) sts. Divide sts among 4 needles. Join for working in the rnd, being careful not to twist sts; use the gap between the needles and the tail from the CO to keep track of the beginning of rnd. Begin 2x1 Rib in-the-Rnd; work even until piece measures 2" from the beginning.

Shape Sleeve

Note: Change to 12" circ needle when necessary for number of sts on needle. When you change to the circ needle, be sure to place marker for beginning of rnd.
Next Rnd: Change to larger dpns and St st (knit every rnd). Increase 2 sts this rnd, then every 10 (7, 5, 4, 4, 3) rnds 6 (8, 12, 17, 18, 25) times, as follows: M1, knit to last st, M1, k1–83 (87, 98, 108, 116, 130) sts. Work even until piece measures 11 (11, 11½, 11½, 12, 12)" from the beginning. Break yarn; place 4 (8, 12, 16, 20, 24) sts from either side of marker on holder for underarm for Left Sleeve. Transfer remaining 75 (71, 74, 76, 76, 82) sts to waste yarn for Left Sleeve. Set aside. Repeat for Right Sleeve.

Yoke

Next Row (RS): Knit across 48 (52, 55, 58, 61, 65) sts for Right Front, 75 (71, 74, 76, 76, 82) sts for Right Sleeve, 99 (105, 110, 118, 123, 129) sts for Back, 75 (71, 74, 76, 76, 82) sts from holder for Left Sleeve, and 48 (52, 55, 58, 61, 65) sts for Left Front–345 (351, 368, 386, 397, 423) sts.
Note: The first few rows after joining the Sleeves will be a bit tight, but continue knitting and they will become easier.
Continuing in St st, work even until piece measures 4" from beginning of Yoke, ending with a RS row.

Shape Yoke

Decrease Row 1 (WS): Change to smaller circ needle. K1 (4, 3, 6, 1, 4), *k2tog, k2; repeat from * to last 0 (3, 1, 4, 0, 3) sts, knit to end–259 (265, 277, 292, 298, 319) sts remain.
Next Row: K3, p1, *k2, p1; repeat from * to last 3 sts, k3.
Next Row: Knit the knit sts and purl the purl sts as they face you. Work even until piece measures 1¾ (2, 2¼, 2¼, 2½, 2½)" from Decrease Row 1, ending with a RS row.
Decrease Row 2 (WS): K3 (2, 3, 2, 1, 2), *k2tog, k1; repeat from * to last 4 (2, 4, 2, 0, 2) sts, knit to end–175 (178, 187, 196, 199, 214) sts remain.
Next Row: K3, p1, *k2, p1; repeat from * to last 3 sts, k3.

Next Row: Knit the knit sts and purl the purl sts as they face you. Work even until piece measures 1¾ (2, 2¼, 2¼, 2½, 2½)" from Decrease Row 2, ending with a RS row.
Decrease Row 3 (WS): K0 (1, 1, 0, 2, 2), *k1, [k2tog] twice; repeat from * to last 0 (2, 1, 1, 2, 2) sts, knit to end–105 (108, 113, 118, 121, 130) sts remain. Place sts on st holder.

Finishing

Button Band

Using larger circ needle, beginning at Left Front neck edge, pick up and knit 3 sts for every 4 rows along Left Front. Begin Garter st (knit every row); work even for 15 rows. BO all sts loosely knitwise. Place markers for 9 buttons, the first ½" from bottom edge, the last ½" from top edge, and the remaining 7 evenly spaced between.

Buttonhole Band

Using larger circ needle, beginning at bottom Right Front edge, pick up and knit 3 sts for every 4 rows along Right Front. Begin Garter st; work even for 15 rows, working buttonholes opposite markers on Row 8, as follows:
Buttonhole Row (RS): [Knit to marker, yo, k2tog] 9 times, knit to end. BO all sts loosely knitwise.

Neckband

Using smaller circ needle, beginning at Right Front neck edge, pick up and knit 8 sts from Buttonhole Band, knit across 105 (108, 113, 118, 121, 130) sts from holder, pick up and knit 8 sts from Button Band–121 (124, 129, 134, 137, 146) sts. Knit 1 row. BO all sts loosely knitwise.

Using Kitchener st (see page 128), graft underarm sts. Block as desired. Sew buttons at markers.

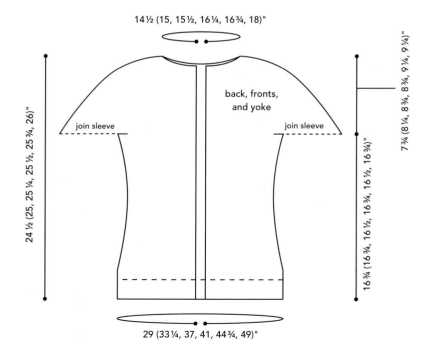

14½ (15, 15½, 16¼, 16¾, 18)"
back, fronts, and yoke
join sleeve
join sleeve
24½ (25, 25¼, 25½, 25¾, 26)"
7¾ (8¼, 8¾, 8¾, 9¼, 9¼)"
16¾ (16¾, 16½, 16¾, 16½, 16¾)"
29 (33¼, 37, 41, 44¾, 49)"
11½ (12, 13½, 15, 16, 16)"
join for yoke
sleeve
11 (11, 11½, 11½, 12, 12)"
9½ (9½, 10, 10, 10¾, 10¾)"

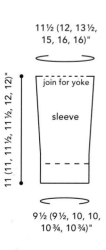

bright stripes blanket

FINISHED MEASUREMENTS
Approximately 50" wide x 55"
long, not including I-Cord Trim

YARN
Farmhouse Yarns Andy's Merino
II (100% merino; 200 yards / 4
ounces): 9 hanks Natural (MC);
2 hanks Lemon Drop (A); 1 hank
each Tangerine (B), Poppy (C),
and Hot Pink (D)

NEEDLES
One 36" (90 cm) long circular (circ)
needle size US 10 ½ (6.5 mm)

One pair double-pointed needles
(dpn) size US 10 (6 mm)

Change needle size if necessary to
obtain correct gauge.

NOTIONS
Four 6" long stitch holders

GAUGE
15 sts and 30 rows (15 ridges) =
4" (10 cm) in Garter st (knit every
row), using larger needles

I've always loved the clean, modern look of bright colors set off by soft, natural white. This blanket is not small, so it does take some time to knit, however if you love garter stitch as much as I do, the knitting is all fun; just stitch away and watch the beautiful colors come together. There is absolutely no sewing involved (really!). It makes a great housewarming gift or could be a special gift for a child's forth birthday (each stripe representing one year) in his or her favorite colors.

Blanket

Side Panel
Using circ needle and MC, CO 140 sts. Begin Garter st (knit every row); work even until piece measures 9" from the beginning, ending with a WS row. Break yarn, leaving sts on needle.

A Panel
*With RS of Side Panel facing, using Cable CO (see page 131) and A, CO 22 sts onto the right-hand end of circ needle.
Row 1 (RS): K21, skp (last st in A together with 1 st in MC), turn work.
Row 2: Knit to end.
Repeat Rows 1 and 2 until all MC sts have been worked, ending with a WS row. Break yarn, transfer sts to st holder.

MC Panel
With RS of A Panel facing, using circ needle and MC, pick up and knit 1 st in every Garter ridge of A Panel—140 sts. Begin Garter st; work even for 3", ending with a WS row. Break yarn, leaving sts on needle.*

Remaining Panels
Repeat from * to * 3 times, replacing A first with B, then with C, then with D, working final repeat of MC Panel even for 9", ending with a WS row. BO all sts loosely.

Finishing

Top Trim

With RS of Blanket facing, using MC and circ needle, pick up and knit 1 st in every Garter ridge of MC Side Panel, *knit across 22 sts on holder for next color Panel, pick up and knit 1 st in every Garter ridge of next MC Panel; repeat from * to end of last MC Panel. Begin Garter st; work even for 9", ending with a WS row. BO all sts loosely.

Bottom Trim

Wth RS of Blanket facing, using MC and circ needle, pick up and knit 1 st for every Garter ridge or CO st along bottom edge of Blanket, making sure to pick up into both strands of Cable CO to avoid gaps. Begin Garter st; work even for 9", ending with a WS row. BO all sts loosely.

I-Cord Trim

Beginning just past one corner of Blanket, work Applied I-Cord around entire edge of Blanket, as follows: Using dpns and A, CO 3 sts; working yarn will be at left-hand side of the needle. *Transfer needle with sts to left hand, bring yarn around behind work to right-hand side; using a second dpn, working sts from right to left and pulling yarn from left to right for the first st, k2, slip 1, pick up and knit 1 st from edge to which I-Cord will be applied). Do not turn; slide sts to opposite end of needle. Repeat from * around entire edge of Blanket. When working around a corner, work 2 rows without picking up a stitch from edge to allow I-Cord to turn corner smoothly. BO all sts. Sew BO edge of I-Cord to CO edge.

Block if desired.

wrapping handknit gifts:
a final flourish

Handknitting a gift is a sincere act of affection, so the gift certainly deserves a special wrapping. But if you're anything like me, you may not have much time leftover for this kind of thoughtfulness once the knitting is done. To help both you and me, my dear friend and business partner Page Marchese Norman developed these quick and easy final flourishes. If you don't have a local source for the supplies required, see page 139.

Sneak Peek Gift Wrap

Glassine adds a bit of shine to your gift plus a sneak peek at what's inside. For this option, you will need a glassine bag that's slightly larger than the gift, a ⅛" hole punch, and three colors of thin yarn that coordinate with or are leftover from your project. Insert the gift, fold the bag's end over, and use the ⅛" hole punch to make three rows of holes approximately ¼" apart (for the package shown, we made 25 holes in each row). Using a tapestry needle, weave yarn through holes.

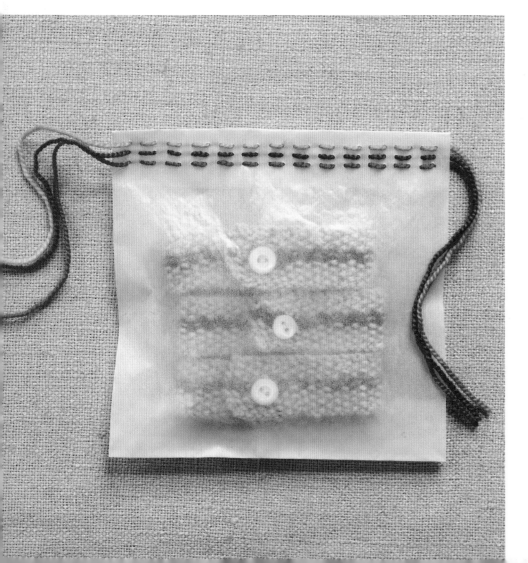

Spectrum Scraps

This idea makes beautiful use of yarn scraps, those small bits that aren't long enough to knit with but are just too beautiful to throw away. To begin, place your gift in a kraft box. Arrange your scraps in a pleasing pattern and tie each length around the box in a square knot (to work a square knot, tie the right length over the left length, then tie the left length over the right); the knots look good at either the top or the bottom of the box. Once you're satisfied with your arrangement, trim the ends of the ties to desired length. To make this wrapping really sing and create depth and texture, vary the colors, gauges, and fibers of the yarns.

Extra-Button Gift Tags

It's always thoughtful to give some extra yarn and an extra button or two (or four!) with a handknitted cardigan or other buttoned item. Trace the template below onto thin paper and cut out. Use your template to cut the shape of the tag from card stock, including the notches to wrap the yarn around. Using a $\frac{1}{6}$" hole punch, make a hole at the top of the tag and tie some yarn through it to make a hanging loop. Using a $\frac{1}{6}$" hole punch, make holes to sew the buttons through, then sew on the buttons with yarn (or cotton thread if your buttons are very small), and tie off on the back of the card. Wrap extra yarn around the card at the notches. Use a pen to write a note or care instructions.

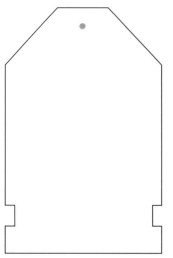

Gift Tag Template

All Buttoned Up Gift Wrap

This wrap is made with a combination of smooth yarns and fuzzy mohair all tied up around a big button; it's a simple idea that is both charming and beautiful. Wrap the box in the paper and secure with clear tape. Tie an assortment of yarn scraps in closely related colors but varying fibers and weights around the box as if they were a standard ribbon, with the ends coming together at the top. Thread the yarn ends through an oversized button from the wrong side, tie the yarn in a square knot (to work a square knot, tie the right length over the left length, then tie the left length over the right). Trim the ends to the desired length.

124

100% ALPACA
PLEASE HAND WASH

To: Bear
♡ love, Joelle

To Novella
love, Joelle

FINISHING TECHNIQUES

I tried to design most of the projects in this book so they require minimal finishing (thus less time). Following are the techniques you need to know.

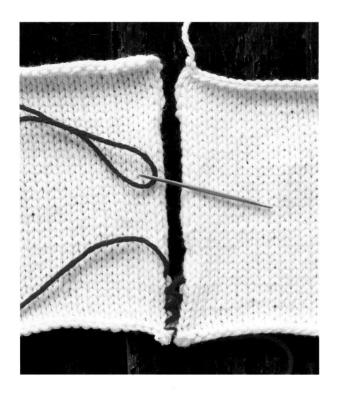

Mattress Stitch

When sewing is required, and it occasionally is no matter how much you plan ahead, I always go for Mattress stitch, which is very simple and practically invisible.

STEP 1: Lay the two pieces to be sewn together right side up. Thread a tapestry needle with the same yarn you used to knit the piece.

STEP 2: Insert the tapestry needle into the front of the very first stitch on one of the two pieces you are sewing together and pull the yarn through, leaving a tail approximately 5" in length; you will weave the tail into the back of your knitting when you are through.

STEP 3: Insert the tapestry needle into the front of the very first stitch on the opposite piece and pull the yarn through.

STEP 4: Insert the tapestry needle from the right side into the same stitch you started in when working Step 2 above, and underneath the two horizontal bars connecting the edge stitch to the next stitch, bringing the tapestry needle back to the front of work.

STEP 5: Insert the tapestry needle from the right side into the stitch on the opposite side where the yarn exited last time, and underneath the two horizontal bars connecting the edge stitch to the next stitch, bringing the tapestry needle back to the front of work. Repeat this step a few times and pull yarn taut (but not so tight that it buckles the fabric).

Repeat Step 5 until seam is complete.

Picking Up Stitches

I'm nearly always in a hurry, so I try to find ways to construct my patterns so that sewing isn't required at the end. Often, I connect two pieces of a project by picking up stitches on one and then knitting the second piece from there.

Picking Up Stitches from Garter Stitch

As shown above, slip your left-hand needle through the first loop of the bottom-most ridge of knitting, slip your right-hand needle underneath the left-hand needle, wrap the yarn around the right-hand needle and knit the stitch as usual. You'll have one stitch on your right-hand needle. Continue up the work, picking up one stitch for every ridge of knitting.

Picking Up Stitches from Stockinette Stitch

This technique is as simple as picking up from Garter stitch, but the challenge is where to pick up from. I always pick up through the "v" of the stitch next to the edge (rather than through the edge itself or between stitches) with my left-hand needle, and then, as shown below, insert the right-hand needle under the left-hand needle, wrap the yarn around the right-hand needle and knit as usual. With Stockinette stitch, I find that you need to pick up 3 out of every 4 rows to create a smooth edge; any more than that and your edge will have too many stitches. This technique is useful for picking up stitches around armholes, necklines, and for button bands.

Kitchener Stitch

Kitchener stitch is a technique for invisibly weaving together live stitches. It is one of my favorite finishing techniques for producing professional and practically invisible results. The photo at left shows Kitchener stitch worked in contrasting yarn so that you can see what it does. Knitters tend to shy away from learning this stitch because the technique seems complicated when it's all written out, but it's actually very simple to do; the only real challenge is keeping track of where you are in the steps.

STEP 1: Thread a tapestry needle with the same yarn you used to work your project. Hold the needles with live stitches parallel in your left hand. Insert the tapestry needle through the first stitch on the front needle as if to purl (photo A), pull the yarn through, leaving a tail approximately 5" long; you will weave the tail in later. Leave the stitch on the front needle.

STEP 2: Insert the tapestry needle through the first stitch on the back needle as if to knit (photo B), pull the yarn through, leaving the stitch on the back needle.

STEP 3: Insert the tapestry needle through the first stitch on the front needle as if to knit (photo C), pull the yarn through, removing the stitch from the front needle.

STEP 4: Insert the tapestry needle through the first stitch on the front needle as if to purl (photo A), pull the yarn through, leaving the stitch on the front needle.

STEP 5: Insert the tapestry needle through the first stitch on the back needle as if to purl (photo D), pull the yarn through, removing the stitch from the back needle.

STEP 6: Insert the tapestry needle through the first stitch on the back needle as if to knit (photo B), pull the yarn through, leaving the stitch on the back needle.

Repeat Steps 4-6 until all stitches have been worked. Every few stitches, adjust the tension of your work, making sure not to pull too tightly. Remember, you are making an extra row of knitting rather than sewing together a seam.

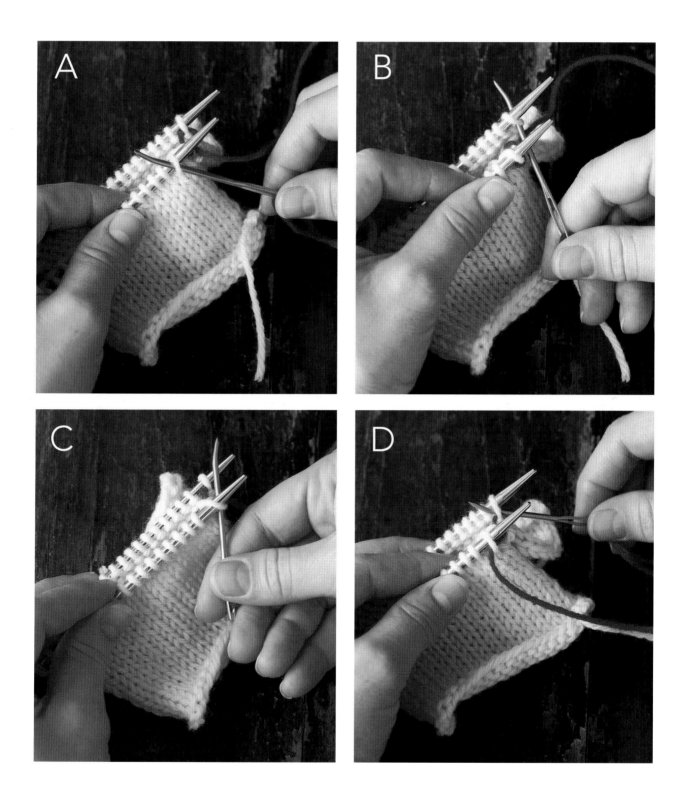

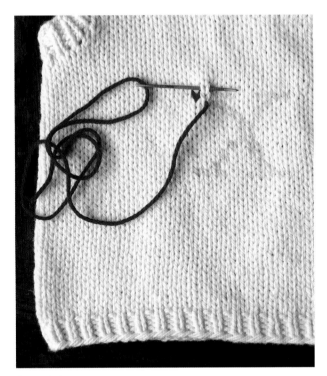

Steps 1-4

Duplicate Stitch

Duplicate stitch is one of my favorite ways to embellish a project. It looks so professional, even if you do it as an afterthought!

STEP 1: Following a chart (or drawing freehand), use a water-soluble disappearing fabric marker to mark the stitches you intend to stitch over.

STEP 2: Thread the tapestry needle with desired yarn; do not tie a knot at the end of yarn.

STEP 3: Insert the needle from the wrong side of the fabric, into the bottom of the "v" of the first marked stitch on the left-hand side of the drawn motif, pull the yarn through to the front, leaving a tail on the inside of the work approximately 5" long, to be sewn into the back of work when you are through.

STEP 4: Insert the needle from the front of the work underneath both strands of the stitch above the first marked stitch as pictured, pull the yarn through.

STEP 5: Insert the needle back into the bottom of the "v" of the first marked stitch and out of the bottom of the "v" of the next stitch to the right.

Repeat Steps 4 and 5 until you are through.

Note: Sometimes you have to insert the tapestry needle underneath a stitch that has already been "duplicated" to make a row of vertical stitches. When you do this, be sure to go under both the duplicate yarn and the original yarn for best results.

OTHER TECHNIQUES AND ABBREVIATIONS

BO	Bind off
Cable CO (at beginning of row)	*Where indicated in pattern, insert the tip of the right-hand needle into the space between the last 2 sts on the left-hand needle and draw up a loop; place the loop on the left-hand needle. Repeat from * for remaining sts to be CO.
Circ	Circular
Cn	Cable needle
CO	Cast on
Dpn(s)	Double-pointed needle(s)
K1-f/b	Knit into front loop and back loop of same stitch to increase 1 stitch.
K1-tbl	Knit 1 stitch through back loop.
K2tog	Knit 2 sts together.
K	Knit
Long-Tail **(Thumb) CO**	Leaving tail with about 1" of yarn for each st to be cast on, make a slipknot in the yarn and place it on the right-hand needle, with the end to the front and the working end to the back. Insert the thumb and forefinger of your left hand between the strands of yarn so that the working end is around your forefinger, and the tail end is around your thumb "slingshot" fashion; *insert the tip of the right-hand needle into the front loop on the thumb, hook the strand of yarn coming from the forefinger from back to front, and draw it through the loop on your thumb; remove your thumb from the loop and pull on the working yarn to tighten the new st on the right-hand needle; return your thumb and forefinger to their original positions, and repeat from * for remaining sts to be CO.
M1 or M1-l (make 1-left slanting)	With tip of left-hand needle inserted from front to back, lift strand between 2 needles onto left-hand needle; knit strand through back loop to increase 1 stitch.
M1-p (make 1 purlwise)	With tip of left-hand needle inserted from back to front, lift strand between 2 needles onto left-hand needle; purl strand through front loop to increase 1 stitch.

M1-r **(make 1-right slanting)**	With tip of left-hand needle inserted from back to front, lift strand between 2 needles onto left-hand needle; knit strand through front loop to increase 1 stitch.
P2tog	Purl 2 sts together.
Pm	Place marker
Provisional **(Crochet Chain) CO**	Using a crochet hook and smooth waste yarn (crochet cotton or ravel cord used for machine knitting), work a crochet chain with a few more chains than the number of sts needed; fasten off. If desired, tie a knot on the fastened-off end to mark the end that you will be unraveling from later. Turn the chain over; with a needle 1 size smaller than required for piece and working yarn, starting a few chains in from the beginning of the chain, pick up and knit one st in each bump at the back of the chain until you have the required number of CO sts, leaving any extra chains at the end unworked. Change to needle size required for project on first row.
P	Purl
Psso (pass slipped **stitch over)**	Pass slipped st on right-hand needle over sts indicated in instructions, as in binding off.
Rnd(s)	Round(s)
RS	Right side
Short Row Shaping	Work the number of sts specified in the instructions, wrap and turn (wrp-t) as follows: To wrap a knit st, bring yarn to the front (purl position), slip the next st purlwise to the right-hand needle, bring yarn to the back of work, return the slipped st on the right-hand needle to the left-hand needle purlwise; turn, ready to work the next row, leaving the remaining sts unworked. To wrap a purl stitch, work as for wrapping a knit st, but bring yarn to the back (knit position) before slipping the stitch, and to the front after slipping the stitch. When short rows are completed, or when working progressively longer short rows, work the wrap together with the wrapped st as you come to it as follows: If st is to be worked as a knit st, insert the right-hand needle into the wrap, from below, then into the wrapped st; k2tog; if st to be worked is a purl st, insert needle into the wrapped st, then down into the wrap; p2tog. (Wrap may be lifted onto the left-hand needle, then worked together with the wrapped st if this is easier.)
Skp **(slip, knit, pass)**	Slip next st knitwise to right-hand needle, k1, pass slipped st over knit st.

Sk2p (double decrease)	Slip next st knitwise to right-hand needle, k2tog, pass slipped st over st from k2tog.
Sm	Slip marker
Ssk (slip, slip, knit)	Slip next 2 sts to right-hand needle one at a time as if to knit; return them to left-hand needle one at a time in their new orientation; knit them together through back loops.
Ssp (slip, slip, purl)	Slip next 2 sts to right-hand needle one at a time as if to knit; return them to left-hand needle one at a time in their new orientation; purl them together through the back loops.
St(s)	Stitch(es)
Tbl	Through back loop
Three-Needle BO	Place the sts to be joined onto 2 same-sized needles; hold the pieces to be joined with the RSs facing each other and the needles parallel, both pointing to the right. Holding both needles in your left hand, using working yarn and a third needle same size or 1 size larger, insert third needle into first st on front needle, then into first st on back needle; knit these 2 sts together; *knit next st from each needle together (2 sts on right-hand needle); pass first st over second st to BO 1 st. Repeat from * until 1 st remains on third needle; cut yarn and fasten off.
Tog	Together
WS	Wrong side
Wrp-t	Wrap and turn
Wyib	With yarn in back
Wyif	With yarn in front
Yb	Yarn back
Yf	Yarn front
Yo	Yarnover

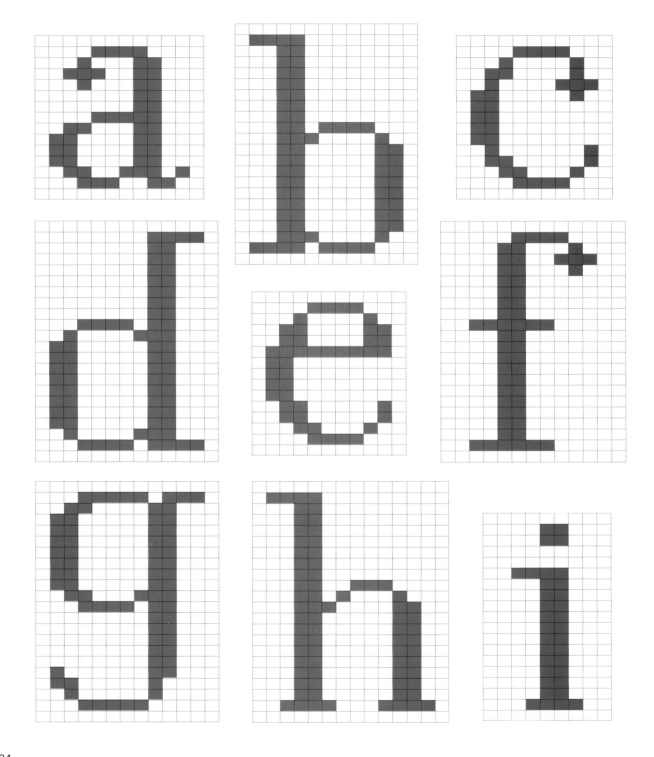

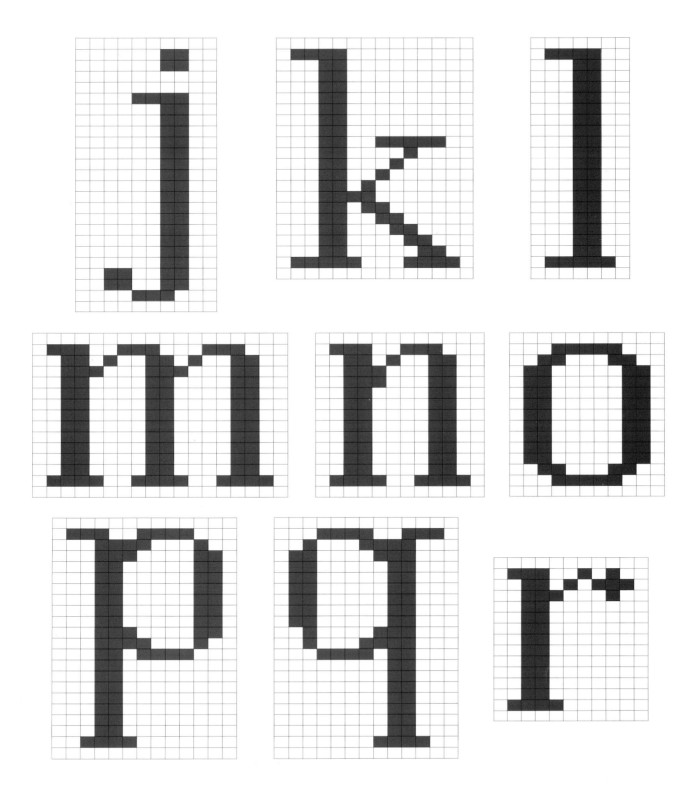

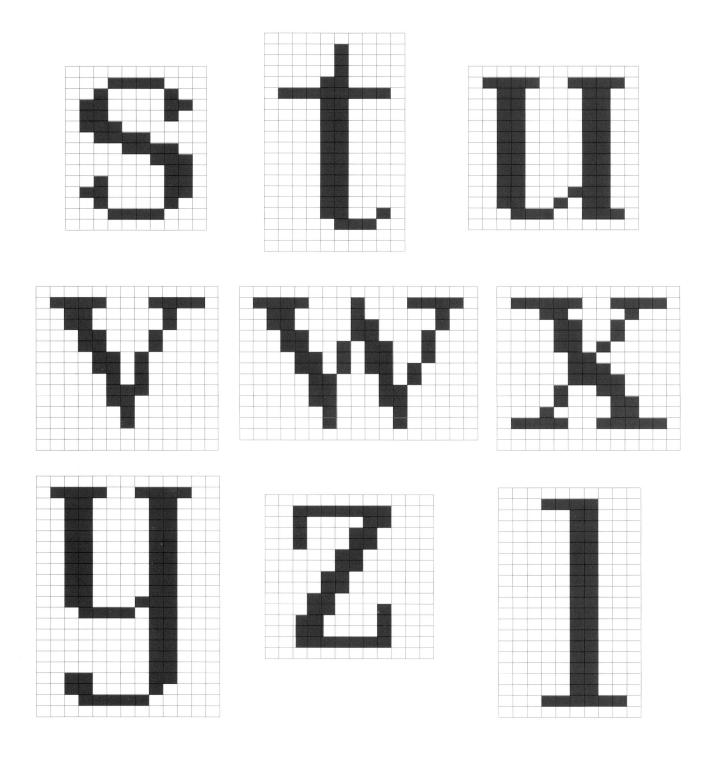

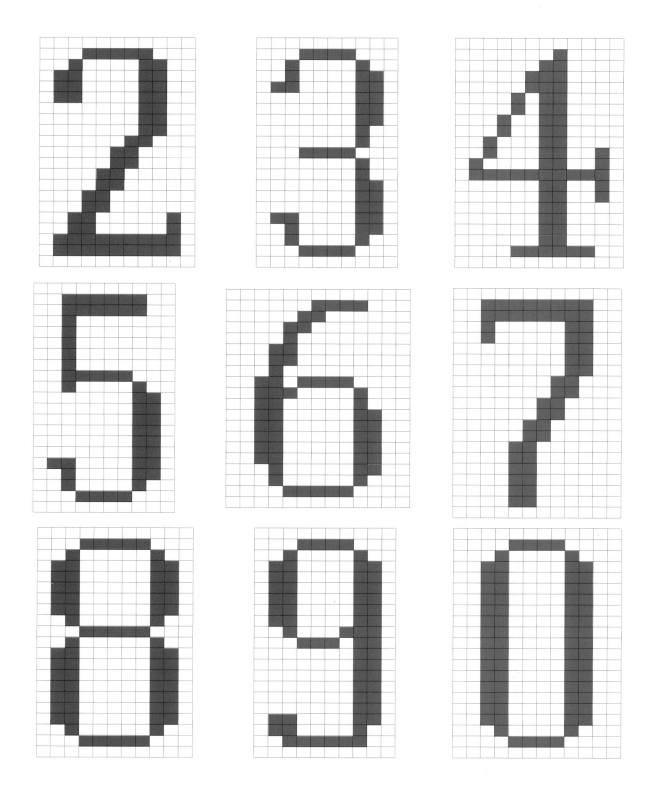

SOURCES FOR SUPPLIES

All yarn and knitting supplies featured in this book are available from:

Purl Soho
459 Broome Street
New York, NY 10013
www.purlsoho.com

To find a local source for the yarn and other supplies featured in this book, contact the distributors below:

Alchemy Yarns of Transformation
www.alchemyyarns.com

Belangor
Joseph Galler
800 836 3314

Blue Sky Alpacas
www.blueskyalpacas.com

Cascade Yarns
www.cascadeyarns.com

Farmhouse Yarns
www.farmhouseyarns.com

The Fibre Company
www.thefibreco.com

Hand Jive and Nature's Palette Yarns
www.handjiveknits.com

Jade Sapphire
www.jadesapphire.com

Koigu Wool Designs
www.koigu.com

Lobster Pot Yarns
215 499 7284

Lorna's Laces
www.lornaslaces.net

Louet
www.louet.com

Manos del Uruguay
www.fairmountfibers.com

Spud & Chloë
www.spudandchloe.com

Wagtail Yarns
www.wagtailyarns.com

Specialty Craft Items:

Fiskars Hole Punches
www.fiskars.com

Kraft Paper Boxes
Mason Box Company
www.masonbox.com

Dried Lavender
LocalHarvest
www.localharvest.org

Glassine Bags and Gift Wrap
Paper Source
www.paper-source.com

ACKNOWLEDGMENTS

Craft books are never the work of a single individual. Although I may be the official author of this book, there were many other eyes, hands, and minds involved. When I look through the pages I see a record of an arduous and meaningful journey with an incredible team of people who are also my dear friends, and I feel extremely lucky.

As was true for my first two books, this book is the brainchild of my editor and friend Melanie Falick. When Melanie approached me to do this book, shortly after I told her I simply couldn't write another book (ever again!), I put up some resistance, but because I trust her so much, I knew that I would do it in the end. Whenever I'm stuck or my attention wanders, Melanie knows what to say to get me moving again, and this is no small task. With two shops and a retail website to run, I can be a hard person to pin down, but somehow Melanie always manages to do it, and she always gets me to do my best work. But more than that, I would not be capable of writing even one word if I didn't know that Melanie would look over my work with a kind and gentle yet firm and precise editor's eye. So, it goes without saying that if it weren't for Melanie, you wouldn't be reading this book. Thank you, Melanie.

Sue McCain was the technical editor on this book. Sue's eye for detail and knowledge of knitting and knitting language is astonishing and so it gave me a great sense of security and freedom to have her there to oversee my patterns. Editing knitting patterns is not a simple matter, and I was constantly amazed by Sue's ability to hunt down errors, size everything properly, and deal with my constantly wandering attention! I am also grateful to Robin Melanson, who proofed all of the patterns once the book was in layout. It was very reassuring to have an extra set of expert eyes reviewing these pages.

Throughout the writing of this book, I had the love and support of two very special people: my business partners at Purl, Purl Patchwork, and purlsoho.com, Jennifer Hoverson Jahnke and Page Marchese Norman. As I toiled over the book, I let lots of other things in our business fall through the cracks. Thankfully, they were both there to catch what I couldn't handle, and much more. Knowing they were there allowed me the time and mental space I needed to do a good job. In addition, both Jen and Page contributed in less abstract ways. Jen helped knit samples of the Beret, the Very Pretty Lace Scarf, countless Family Ribbed Hats, and swatches for the how-to photos. I left all of my unfinished knitting in her hands during the photo shoot, and as I knew she would, she came through and finished everything with ample time to spare. Jen is nothing if not a lightning-fast knitter! Jen also modeled both her beautiful face and her last-minute airport-manicured hands. Page sat me down one stressful day when I was sure I couldn't come up with even one original wrapping idea and brainstormed with me. She made the impeccable wrapping projects in the last chapter, and they are far more thoughtful and complete than anything I could have done given the amount of work I had left to finish before the deadline. Page also focused me on pulling together the numerous props and backgrounds that you see in these photos, and made sure that everything and everyone was organized and ready for the shoot. Page's attention to detail made it possible for all of us involved to focus our energy on being creative and totally inspired.

As with my two other books, *Last-Minute Knitted Gifts* and *Last-Minute Patchwork + Quilted Gifts*, one of my most cherished friends, Anna Williams, took all of the beautiful photos. Anna is an amazingly gifted photographer (as well as an incredibly generous and lovely person) so I was both delighted and grateful that she made time in her very busy schedule to work with me again. Before the shoot, Anna asked me if I wanted to go digital for this book, which I had never done on a professional project before. If it had been anyone else asking, I don't know if I would have been comfortable making such a big leap (for me) on such a big project, but with Anna I knew I could trust that the work would be just as beautiful digitally as it would have been on film. And what a revelation it was; the freedom and speed of working digitally allowed us to really stretch ourselves and make every single photograph a favorite. Also, the experience of learning about the digital process from such a generous friend was exciting as well as inspiring. I would also like to give special thanks to Jeff Denton for his wonderful retouching.

In addition to designing the beautiful layouts for this book, Brooke Hellewell Reynolds contributed her many talents as an art director, organizer, and very dear friend. I've worked with Brooke for a long time on many different projects, so whenever she gets involved in my books (she also worked very closely with me on my second book, *Last-Minute Patchwork + Quilted Gifts*) I can relax in the knowledge that we speak the same language and that almost nothing will be overlooked. During the photo shoot for this book, Brooke was never shy about pushing our team to go the extra step or get the extra shot, and I think this is one of the reasons why this book feels so complete. One of my fondest memories from the shoot is listening to Brooke and Page talk passionately about how much they loved the colors as they set up the rainbow of yarns on pages 6 and 7.

We took all of the photos in rural New York State, in a town where you can't exactly order in food for everyone! But we had two very special people to keep our crew fed and happy. For our first shoot, friend and longtime coworker Molly Schnick lovingly prepared our delicious meals. For the second shoot, my youngest sister, Sara Hoverson, whom I am very proud of for recently becoming an official professional chef, came all the way from Ohio to cook for us. Both Sara and Molly took on a pretty big challenge (just imagine if you will, a house full of New York City food lovers with lots of different dietary needs and restrictions) and they both did an amazing job.

There are three patterns in this book that deserve special mention. Leah Mitchell designed and created the Toe-Up Socks on page 107 as well as Leah's Lovely Cardigan on page 111. Both of these patterns are incredibly thoughtful, detailed, and beautiful, just like Leah. While we collaborated on the general idea for the socks, Leah took the pattern to another level by researching toes, heels, yarns, and stitch patterns. Her cardigan is her unique design, one she made for herself that I fell in love with the minute I saw it! I am so pleased that she allowed me to publish it here. My longtime friend Kelly McKaig created Kelly's Mittens on page 59. In addition to this pattern, Kelly has created several patterns for me over the years, including Kelly's Pincushions in *Last-Minute Patchwork + Quilted Gifts*. Kelly's ability to knit mittens was my original inspiration to learn more than garter-stitch rectangles, and I feel thankful for her inspiration just about every time I pick up my needles! Having her mitten pattern in this book makes me happy not only because it is such a lovely pattern, but also because I'm very attached to them sentimentally.

Knitting for a photo shoot deadline is intense, especially when all of the projects are due almost all at once, and help is most definitely required! A special thanks to Jennifer Hoverson Jahnke, Finlay Logan, Calia Talmor, Leah Mitchell, and Faye Rubenstein for all of the energy and care they put into very last-minute knitting for this book. Additionally, throughout the creation of this book our business had lots of support from our staff, including Sophie Dorsey, Eva Jensen, Mari T. Kirsten, Finlay Logan, Shantilal Mehta, Jeanne Moro, Debbie Murai, Rickie Painter, Faye Rubenstein, Molly Schnick, Nicole Egana Stadler, Calia Talmor, Whitney Van Nes, and Jeremy Wilson. And last, but certainly not least, a very special thanks to our models: Mason Adams, Novella Adams, Adrianna Florke, Jacob Florke (and the eggs from his chickens), Jennifer Hoverson Jahnke, Sara Hoverson, Coco Norman, Adam Ogilvie, Bear Ogilvie, Brooke Hellewell Reynolds, Molly Schnick, Whitney Van Nes, and Anna Williams.

INDEX